CW00429716

About the authors

David Booth is a research fellow at the Overseas Development Institute. Prior to this, he was a university academic at Hull and Swansea, latterly as professor of development studies. He has been editor of the journal *Development Policy Review* (2000–09) and director of the Africa Power and Politics Programme (2007–12). He now coordinates a joint project on Developmental Regimes in Africa while also contributing to training courses in applied political economy analysis for development agencies worldwide. David's publications include *Rethinking Social Development* (1994), *Fighting Poverty in Africa: Are PRSPs Making a Difference?* (2003), *Good Governance, Aid Modalities and Poverty Reduction* (2008), *Working with the Grain? Rethinking African Governance* (2011) and *Development as a Collective Action Problem* (2012). He has authored numerous journal articles, ODI papers and blogs in related fields.

Diana Cammack is a research associate of the Overseas Development Institute. She obtained her PhD at the University of California, specialising in South African history (*The Road to War*, 1990). As an SSRC-MacArthur Fellow on Peace and Security in a Changing World she retrained at Oxford University in the early 1990s in human rights and the politics of aid. Diana led the politics and governance team at the Overseas Development Institute for three years and between 2008 and 2012 she headed the Local Governance and Leadership stream of the Africa Power and Politics Programme. She has worked as a consultant researcher in sub-Saharan Africa for three decades. In recent years she has specialised in political economy studies, with a focus on the link between politics and development in neopatrimonial and fragile states.

GOVERNANCE FOR DEVELOPMENT IN AFRICA

SOLVING COLLECTIVE ACTION PROBLEMS

David Booth and Diana Cammack

Zed Books
LONDON | NEW YORK

Governance for Development in Africa: Solving collective action problems
was first published in 2013 by Zed Books Ltd, 7 Cynthia Street, London N1
9JF, UK and Room 400, 175 Fifth Avenue, New York, NY 10010, USA

www.zedbooks.co.uk

Copyright © David Booth and Diana Cammack 2013

The rights of David Booth and Diana Cammack to be identified as the
authors of this work have been asserted by them in accordance with the
Copyright, Designs and Patents Act, 1988

Set in Monotype Plantin and FFKievit by Ewan Smith,
London NW5
Index: ed.emery@thefreeuniversity.net
Cover design: www.roguefour.co.uk
Printed and bound in Great Britain by CPI Group (UK) Ltd,
Croydon, CRO 4YY

Distributed in the USA exclusively by Palgrave Macmillan, a division of
St Martin's Press, LLC, 175 Fifth Avenue, New York, NY 10010, USA

All rights reserved. No part of this publication may be reproduced,
stored in a retrieval system or transmitted in any form or by any means,
electronic, mechanical, photocopying or otherwise, without the prior
permission of Zed Books Ltd.

A catalogue record for this book is available from the British Library
Library of Congress Cataloging in Publication Data available

ISBN 978 1 78032 595 8 hb
ISBN 978 1 78032 594 1 pb

CONTENTS

Figures and boxes | vi
Abbreviations | vii Acknowledgements | ix
Approximate exchange rates | xi

Introduction 1

1 From 'good governance' to governance that works . . . 9

2 The country contexts 31

3 Maternal health: why is Rwanda doing better than
   Malawi, Niger and Uganda?. 41

4 The politics of policy incoherence and provider
   indiscipline. 73

5 The space for local problem-solving and practical
   hybridity 97

Conclusion 122

Bibliography | 140
Index | 155

FIGURES AND BOXES

Figures

3.1 Maternal mortality ratios (deaths per 100,000 live births) 44
3.2 Deliveries at health facility 44

Boxes

0.1 Public goods and merit goods explained. 7
1.1 What is 'good governance'? 9
1.2 The principal–agent framework 12
1.3 Collective action and anti-corruption 16
1.4 The 'free-rider problem' explained 17

ABBREVIATIONS

APPP	Africa Power and Politics Programme
BTC	Belgian Technical Cooperation
CEO	Chief Executive Officer
CHRAJ	Commission on Human Rights and Administrative Justice
CHW	Community Health Worker (Rwanda)
DC	District Commissioner
DfID	Department for International Development (UK)
DHS	Demographic and Health Survey
DPP	Democratic Progressive Party (Malawi)
DRC	Democratic Republic of Congo/Development Research Centre (UK)
FCFA	CFA franc
HIPC	Heavily Indebted Poor Countries (debt relief initiative)
HIV	Human Immune-deficiency Virus
HSA	Health Surveillance Assistant (Malawi)
LASDEL	Laboratoire d'études et de recherches sur les dynamiques sociales et le développement local (Niger and Benin)
MCP	Malawi Congress Party
MHSDMU	Medicines and Health Service Delivery Monitoring Unit (Uganda)
MMR	maternal mortality ratio
MP	Member of Parliament
MRND	Mouvement républicain national pour la démocratie et le développement (Rwanda)
NGO	non-governmental organisation
PPP	Purchasing Power Parity (exchange rate)
RPF	Rwandan Patriotic Front
TBA	traditional birth attendant
UDF	United Democratic Front (Malawi)
UN	United Nations
WDR	World Development Report
WHO	World Health Organization

ACKNOWLEDGEMENTS

This book is the fruit of a large collective effort. The joint authors owe a huge debt to the field researchers who collected much of the information and insights on which we draw, often under conditions of discomfort, weariness and occasionally (we do not doubt) tedium. More particularly, we have made heavy use of their field reports as well as the field notes and working papers drafted by the country team leaders of APPP's Local Governance and Leadership research stream. We are also indebted to APPP's associated PhD researchers and to the coordinators of two other APPP programmes of work: the Local Justice and the Parental Preferences and Religious Education streams. We were frequently inspired by the researchers whose contributions were mainly in APPP's other research streams as well as by its able and committed managers and communicators.

Those to be thanked in these various categories make a long list: Fabien Affo, Abdelkader Aghali, Sewor Aikins, Mahaman Tidjani Alou, Djibo Amadou, James Amani, Charles Ankisiba, Kojo Asante, Winnifred Babirye, Dennis Bataringaya, Isaline Bergamaschi, Giorgio Blundo, Mamadou Bodian, Yerima Borgui, Victor Brobbey, Vikki Chambers, Sidy Cissokho, Brian Cooksey, Richard C. Crook, Charlotte Cross, Martin Dawson, Aissa Diarra, Theodore Dzeble, Jean Enam, Denis Pompidou Folefack, Mesfin Gebremichael, Frederick Golooba-Mutebi, Veronica Temesio Gómez, Chililo O. Gondwe, E. Gyimah-Boadi, Yvonne Habiyonizeye, Moussa Ibrahim Hassan, Ross Herbert, Goran Hyden, Abdourahmane Idrissa, Younoussi Issa, Tina Maria Jensen, Rosemary Kaduru, Désiré Kamanzi, Jonathan Kaminski, Edge Kanyongolo, Andrew Kawooya Ssebunya, Tim Kelsall, Bourema Kone, Ashley E. Leinweber, Staffan I. Lindberg, Charles Lwanga-Ntale, James Manor, Sue Martin, Marion Mbabazi, Vitima Mkandawire, John Bosco Mubiru, Beatrice Mugambe, Jean-Claude Mugunga, Edward Munyaburanga, Patricia Mupeta, Winnie Musoke, Basileke Mwamlima, Annet Nannungi, Joel Nkhonya, Levy Odera, George Ofosu, Jean-Pierre Olivier de Sardan, Tam O'Neil, Amadou

Oumarou, Winifred Pankani, Alina Rocha Menocal, Bernard Sabiti, Edem Selormey, Renata Serra, Sonia Sezille, Ursula Stelman, Dorothy Tetteh, Gideon Tetteh, Véronique Theriault, Soulemane Thiam, Sarah Vaughan, Leonardo Villalón, Moir Walita Mkandawire, Anna Workman, Konnie Zimba and Eveness Zuze.

We should also like to express appreciation to the hundreds of government officials, politicians, parastatal managers, professional staffs, chiefs and other local leaders, NGO workers and local residents, in all of the places we worked between 2008 and 2012. They were with few exceptions welcoming, patient and unstinting in their willingness to spend time answering our enquiries and providing the information and insights upon which this book is substantially based.

APPP was a consortium research programme funded by the Research and Evidence Division of the UK Department for International Development and Irish Aid for the benefit of developing countries. Continuing support to the APPP website and to follow-up research is being provided by the Netherlands Ministry of Foreign Affairs under the Developmental Regimes in Africa project. We are grateful to those who have provided us with advisory support on behalf of the three funders, including Richard Thomas, Max Everest-Phillips, Helen Richards and Tom Wingfield at DfID; Nicole McHugh, Kevin Carroll and Donal Cronin at Irish Aid; and Martin Koper, Marten de Boer and Roel van der Veen in The Hague. Finally, we were well served by APPP's Consortium Advisory Group: Thomas Bierschenk, Patrick Chabal, Jane Harrigan, Adrian Leftwich, Stephen Ndegwa and Ole Therkildsen. Of course, none of these organisations or individuals is responsible in any way for what we have written.

Some parts of the book, especially Chapter 1, draw heavily on sections of the APPP general synthesis report (Booth 2012a). Elsewhere, we have reworked material that has previously appeared in one or another of APPP's publications or unpublished field reports. In these cases, we acknowledge the source with gratitude and invite readers to consult the original documents for further details.

APPROXIMATE EXCHANGE RATES
(US$, END OF 2010)

Malawi kwacha 152
CFA franc 497
Rwandan franc 575
Uganda shilling 2,335

INTRODUCTION

Anyone working for more than a few years in the 'development business' will tell you that a great deal of what they do fails. This is because much of the effort expended in support of development in the world's poorest countries is predicated on false assumptions about how progress happens in human societies. Over the last two decades, development work has been based on the view that good governance – taken as the system with which countries of the global North currently regulate their affairs – provides a universally valid prescription for economic transformation and social advance. More especially, it is argued that economic development arises from democracy, where democracy is taken to imply not just regular elections but also accountability of government to the people, rule of law, effective corruption controls and a responsive and professional state bureaucracy. This ahistorical view takes insufficient notice of the fact that Western states did not become economic powerhouses (from the 1750s onwards), and that China and the Asian Tigers did not grow their economies in the twentieth century, by adopting good governance institutions. Full-blown capitalism creates the social structures and organisational capabilities that lead to democratic governance, not the other way around (Sandbrook 1985; Chang 2007a; North et al. 2009).

This is not to say that democracy is not worth having, but only that real democracy is not an available option in most of Africa. South of the Sahara and north of the Limpopo, Africa barely has an entrepreneurial middle class. And where most development aid is targeted – at Africa's poorest countries – a different, not-yet-capitalist, class structure exists and a distinct type of political system operates, one that is sometimes called democratic because elections are held but fails to qualify on most other criteria. This essential fact tends to be ignored when well-meaning outsiders and their local allies invest their hopes in a strategy of building electoral systems and 'civil societies' so that citizens can begin to hold politicians and public servants accountable for delivering public services and facilitating growth. A further flight into unreality is taken when populations of largely rural people are treated as actors in a simple democratic drama where as principal players they 'demand good governance' from political leaders and officials, the latter conceived as their 'agents'.

Discovering institutions for African development

For the five years 2007–12, the Africa Power and Politics Programme (APPP) was in the field documenting what actually happens on the ground: what sorts of institutions and what forms of governance are really effective in improving the delivery of key public goods in low-income sub-Saharan Africa (hereafter Africa). This search was based on the belief that things are likely to work better if the institutions framing development efforts are appropriate to their context – if they work with the grain of the society – even if they may seem 'second best' in terms of current ideas among politicians and voters in the North.

This book brings together the findings of several APPP research teams whose particular focus was on the delivery of basic public goods. It is the companion to a previously published volume on the topic of state–business relationships and economic transformation (Kelsall 2013). The Local Governance and Leadership team concerned itself with factors influencing public provision in four areas – safe mother-hood, water and sanitation, markets and the enterprise environment, and public order and security. It supported individual research in rural or peri-urban settings in a total of eight African states, with more extensive, collective fieldwork in Malawi, Niger, Rwanda and Uganda. Other research teams investigated local justice provision and educational reforms in Ghana and other countries of West Africa. The common question asked was: which governance institutions work to improve quality and address bottlenecks in public goods provision and why?

Not surprisingly, few outstanding successes were found – which is consistent with other evidence suggesting that basic public goods provision remains shockingly bad in these very poor countries. However, the findings also pointed clearly enough to what helps and what does not in addressing the major blockages in provision. Progress happens when the relevant actors succeed in overcoming the problems that ordinarily prevent them acting in their collective best interest. The way elites respond to collective action challenges at the national level makes the difference between countries where key bottlenecks are dealt with and countries where they are not.

Blockages can be overcome at sub-national level in ways that enhance results, but only where there is space for locally anchored solutions, including solutions that are practical hybrids of technically advanced and locally rooted ways of doing things. The development business is often an obstacle to realising these potentials. It tends to override local solutions, in part because it is easier to use off-the-shelf solutions and partly because of its addiction to ahistorical 'principal–agent' versions of how progress happens. This book explains how and what needs to be done.

Some readers may question our starting assumptions that public goods provision is a central challenge for African development and that current rates of improvement are insufficient. Is not Africa in spite of everything one of the fastest-growing parts of the world economy today? Have there not been historically unprecedented breakthroughs in several fields of human development in recent decades? Some words are needed on these important topics before providing a fuller summary of the argument and structure of the book.

Has African development turned a corner?

It is true that most countries in sub-Saharan Africa are now registering fast and sustained economic growth. This recent growth, which stands in sharp contrast with the stagnation that extended from the end of the 1970s to the mid-1990s, seems, moreover, to be something more than an extended natural-resource boom fuelled by the economic rise of China. The turnaround since the mid-to-late 1990s marks an important shift in the region's fortunes, a fact that has been rightly celebrated (McKinsey Global Institute 2010; Radelet 2010). Arguably, it shows that significant progress can be made without substantial improvements in governance or the effectiveness of states in supplying public goods to their business communities and populations.

We think that is too simple. As Kelsall (2013) points out, recent economic growth in Africa has serious shortcomings. In most countries, it is not having a large impact on mass poverty, mainly because it is not rooted in agricultural productivity gains. It is not leading to a diversification of production and exports or to the acquisition of technological capabilities by new generations of productive enterprises. Much of the current growth is jobless growth, a fatal feature given that sub-Saharan Africa's population is expected to rise from 800 million today to 2.5 billion within a generation, with over one half of the total living in cities (Mills and Herbst 2012: 18–19). In short, economic growth is not leading to the needed structural transformation.

As Kelsall also shows, the countries that are currently showing most promise in economic transformation have some distinctive features in the areas of politics and governance. However, they are not practitioners of conventional good governance, any more than comparable South-East Asian regimes were in an earlier period (van Donge et al. 2012; Vlasblom 2013).

Africa urgently needs to move on from growth to transformation. The key governance factors that affect how this will happen have to do with the nature of the power relationships among members of national elites and the encompassing elite bargain or 'political settlement' (Khan 2010; North et al. 2013). The orthodox prescriptions that limit the state to providing a generally encouraging business climate and some basic public goods are deficient as pointers to the role that governments have played historically in processes of transformation (Noman et al. 2012). In history, the more developmental types of elite bargain, like the more anti-developmental types, centre upon how a country's main sources of economic 'rent' are managed and shared out.

These differences emerge from the ways privileges are allocated among powerful elites; the masses are not significant players on their own behalf. Also, most regimes have significant 'patrimonial' features (that is, the distinction between public assets and the private wealth of the ruling groups is to some extent blurred). We would argue, however, that in history the more developmental regimes have been notable for their attention to the provision of basic public goods – including rural infrastructure and social services – to the population at large. In both North-East and South-East Asia, this feature is what has ensured that processes of economic transformation had the effect of dramatically reducing poverty rates.

Uneven progress in human development

We make no apology, therefore, for giving a central place to basic public provision in this book. But what about the suggestion that African countries are already making good progress in this regard? Again, there is something in this but the real story is more complicated and much less encouraging.

While the global target of the Millennium Development Goals

(MDGs) – to cut in half the rate of world poverty between 1990 and 2015 – was probably already met by 2008, sub-Saharan Africa as a whole is likely to miss most of the MDGs (Mills and Herbst 2012: 12). On the other hand, it has been convincingly argued that the MDGs were set in a way that was not entirely 'fair' to Africa (Vandemoortele 2009). It is also true that some non-income indicators of poverty and well-being have improved significantly even where slow progress has been made in economic and especially agricultural transformation. What has been achieved in this regard is unprecedented by many relevant historical standards (Kenny 2005; Clemens et al. 2007). There is an understandable impulse in the development business to make the most of these gains, to underline that 'Africa can' (Chuhan-Pole and Angwafo 2011) and that 'Africans deserve the credit' (*The Economist*, 2 March 2013: 9).

Drawing attention to development successes, when they happen, is certainly a worthwhile activity. However, realism is also in order, and some other facts need underlining. First, progress on many outcome indicators is extremely uneven across countries and especially between urban and rural areas. Secondly, by the standard of what has been achieved by once very poor countries in Asia since the 1960s, Africa's current progress is not particularly striking. And thirdly, the sectors that have registered the biggest gains are those where a technical fix has been made available and where, after many false starts, international agencies and national authorities have got their act together to provide delivery mechanisms that work. The dramatic reductions achieved in the incidence of several infectious and water-borne diseases are a good example.

These successes, which are mostly in the bio-medical field, have been promoted heavily, and not unreasonably, by those who believe strongly in technical solutions and coordinated international effort. But technical fixes are not available for all fields; nor can it be assumed that what can be achieved by mobilising special organisational efforts provides a template to solve more routine and everyday problems. Anyone who has spent significant time in any sub-Saharan African country knows that routine services and regulation on the ground are often of appalling quality.

There are good reasons, therefore, for a new and urgent emphasis on tackling the outstanding challenges that exist in almost all fields of public goods provision, including both basic services and regulatory public goods such as enforcement of disease-prevention measures. In many of these fields the technical challenges and solutions have been known for a long time. But the institutional and governance arrangements that can deliver those solutions are not well established or properly recognised. APPP was designed to address this gap in knowledge.

Getting to grips with the problem

APPP used a broadened concept of public goods, following the lead of Leonard (2000). That is, the term was taken to embrace not just goods and services characterised by 'non-excludability and non-rivalry' (see Box 0.1), but also a broader range of goods known technically as 'merit goods'. These are goods with strong positive social externalities or side effects that share with public goods proper the tendency to be under-provided by private, market-oriented action. They are particularly important in the field of public health, where the effects of diseases resulting from insufficient care or effort by individuals or households commonly spill over and harm the wider community. The focus on public goods – in this broadened sense – and not just on public *services*, was helpful in recognising the importance of regulatory functions: the enforcement of public health standards, as opposed to curative care, for example.

We combined this broad public goods focus with particular attention to key bottlenecks in delivery. This had an important advantage. It enabled us to deal in a practical way with the fact that indicators of development progress tend to be available only in highly aggregated forms and with long time lags. It was not practical to design the fieldwork around variations in final outcomes (e.g. reductions in maternal or child mortality or growth in rural markets, etc.). On the other hand, we found, it was relatively easy to assess the presence or absence in a particular location of actions to address obvious bottlenecks in provision or regulation.

As indicated above, the aim of the research was to identify what works and what does not in improving the quality of provision of basic public goods. Access and uptake were treated as important dimensions of quality. A particular topic of interest was the wider institutional conditions appearing either to enable or to hinder efforts to address typical bottlenecks in provision. Analysis of the fieldwork findings worked backwards from evidence on the way key bottlenecks

---

Box 0.1 Public goods and merit goods explained

Public goods and merit goods together define a large class of goods (including services) that tend to be under-provided by markets. *Public goods* are defined as those, such as street lighting, which are *non-excludable* (people cannot be excluded from benefits once provided) and *non-rival* (consumption of the good by one does not reduce its availability to others). Unlike public goods proper, *merit goods* such as schools and vaccination programmes are not characterised by non-excludability, but they too tend to be underprovided because the incentives of private suppliers and consumers do not take account of the 'externalities' – for example, the benefits to society of having an educated population or the negative impacts of disease transmission.

---

in provision were being handled in particular places to make inferences about key features of the enabling or inhibiting environment.

Relatively early on in the fieldwork, three strong themes emerged in discussions within the research team about the wider institutional variables affecting the treatment of key bottlenecks:

- the critical importance of whether the de facto policy regime, including organisational mandates and resource flows, in a given sector is internally coherent or not;
- the extent to which the leadership at the national political level motivates and disciplines the multiple actors responsible for the quality of provision, and
- the degree to which there is an environment that promotes or at least permits problem-solving at sub-national levels of the delivery system.

These findings raised in turn questions about the kinds of political processes and regime types that provide a more enabling environment for addressing typical blockages. Pursuing these further issues, our doubts about the dominant approach to improving governance in poor developing countries were confirmed and deepened.

In particular, we were led to the conclusion that the institutional challenges of governance for development are not primarily about one set of people (leaders or citizens) getting another set of people (civil servants or politicians) to be more accountable or otherwise behave in better ways. In other words, they are not to do with either of the variants of the principal–agent perspective that have been the standard fare of the development business for the last twenty years. Both of these underestimate the extent to which actors of all kinds (politicians, officials, service providers *and* ordinary people) face substantial costs and risks when it comes to acting in their collective best interests. Hence, getting better governance for development is first and foremost about finding ways of solving problems of collective action. Principal–agent issues come into the picture eventually but they are embedded in collective action challenges and solutions, not the other way round. This, and its important implications for development action, provides the main theme of this book.

How the book is organised

We begin in Chapter 1 with a fuller statement of the argument sketched above, placing it in the context of broader trends in thinking about governance for development. Chapter 2 provides some background on the four African countries and multiple research sites on which our arguments are primarily based. Chapter 3 focuses on efforts to improve maternal health, providing details and a comparative analysis across all of the countries in which we undertook major collective fieldwork. This chapter shows the importance of the three types of institutional 'blockage' noted previously, and begins to address the question of enabling and inhibiting factors at the political level. Chapter 4 then deepens the discussion with particular attention to the first two of the blockages and what causes them in three of the countries (Malawi, Niger and Uganda), especially with regard to water and sanitation, health services and market management. Turning to the third blockage, Chapter 5 focuses on the factors influencing the scope for local problem-solving and the adoption of practical hybrid solutions. Here we refer to three areas of public goods provision – water, markets and public order – in the context of Malawi and Niger, and to local justice and education services in Ghana and three countries of francophone West Africa. We conclude with a discussion of the implications of the findings, especially for those working to support African development through governance reform or the delivery of aid.

1 | FROM 'GOOD GOVERNANCE' TO GOVERNANCE THAT WORKS

During the last quarter-century, the view has steadily gained ground that if sub-Saharan Africa is to become less poor, it needs to be better governed. But what does that mean? For many people, African and non-African, the answer is obvious: Africa's leaders must be convinced or compelled to practise 'good governance', the elements of which are straightforward and exemplified in the institutions and practices of the democratic capitalist North (see Box 1.1). For some global leaders, this view of matters is self-evident and hardly in need of further justification (e.g. Cameron 2012). However, a growing expert consensus argues that the governance that Africa needs for development is not so easily identified with the good governance template.

This book agrees with that point of view, but also argues that not enough has been done to spell out its implications. It offers a new perspective on what an alternative agenda for governance reform in Africa might contain. It is addressed to governance reformers in Africa as well as to the international development organisations that in one way or another support the cause of improving governance for development in the region and, in the process, heavily influence attitudes and approaches on the ground.

Box 1.1 What is 'good governance'?

According to a typical overview, good governance has eight major characteristics: 'It is participatory, consensus oriented, accountable, transparent, responsive, effective and efficient, equitable and inclusive and follows the rule of law. It assures that corruption is minimized, the views of minorities are taken into account and that the voices of the most vulnerable in society are heard in decision-making. It is also responsive to the present and future needs of society' (UN ESCAP n.d.).

The big debate: from 'best practice' to 'good fit'

The leading edge of thinking about African governance has evolved considerably since the early 1990s, when the concept of good governance was first articulated. The idea that today's Northern institutions provide a suitable template for the governance of development in poor countries is, increasingly, being questioned. According to a view that is now widely adopted, the governance improvements that countries need are specific to time and place. In other words, the historical background against which a reform is attempted and the way it is sequenced with other changes in society and the economy will have a decisive effect on its results.

For these reasons, generic models based on internationally acknowledged 'best practices' (Fukuyama 2004; Levy 2004), or on 'institutional monocropping' (Evans 2004), are likely to prove inappropriate and ineffective. Instead, reformers increasingly recognise that essential institutional functions for economic and social development can be fulfilled in quite varied institutional forms (Chang 2007b; Rodrik 2007a). As the discipline of economics has long recognised in relation to production and markets (Lipsey and Lancaster 1956), what are technically termed 'first-best' solutions are unlikely to be optimal under real-world conditions. By analogy, the governance reforms that work for development may be 'second-best' options in terms of some ideal standard (Rodrik 2007b, 2008). We should stop judging the appropriateness of institutions and proposing governance reforms on the basis of weak theory about the causal linkages between political institutions, especially democratic ones, and development outcomes (Khan 2007; Andrews 2008; Rocha Menocal 2011).

Practitioners are beginning to take this reasoning seriously. It has become accepted in principle that promoters of institutional change should aim to identify reforms that fit the context in which they are working and that prioritise the immediate challenges. That is, external assistance to governance improvement needs to turn its thinking 'upside down', starting from the country reality and how to improve it, rather than from donor ideals, assumptions or preconceptions (Unsworth 2009; Future State 2010). Development agencies should, therefore, encourage their staff to undertake studies of the political economy of the countries and sectors in which they work (DfID 2009; Fritz et al. 2009; Poole 2011; ODI/TPP recurrent). African advocacy groups, for their part, should focus on changes that meet the specific needs and possibilities of their situation, relying less on grand demands that mimic the institutional patterns attained in some of the most economically advanced countries in their very recent history (Grindle 2007; Pritchett et al. 2010).

The APPP research was very much a product of such thinking. Aware that established forms of development support have often been ineffective for the reasons discussed above, we tried to determine what 'working with the grain' would look like, especially in the various contexts that present themselves in Africa today (Crook and Booth 2011). We also picked up the basic idea of a 'good fit' approach and expressed it as 'building on what works' (Booth 2011).

This shift in general ways of thinking is important. But it is not yet clear that the actual practice of international agencies or country reformers has changed very much as a result of it. Overall, development assistance policies are still more about financial transfers than about institutions. And when it comes to institutions, much of the new context-sensitive governance programming looks much like the old kind. This is, at least in part, because even the best donor governance advisers and consultants and the most reflective country activists have real trouble figuring out what to do differently.

There are exceptions, of course, but while the proponents of 'good fit' in governance programming have been moving in the right direction, they are not yet addressing the real challenges of African governance. The idea of basing governance reforms on country realities must be interpreted in a more radical way. The APPP research findings indicate how such an outcome can be achieved.

Principal–agent versus collective action frameworks

Our view is that not all of the reforms customarily offered as examples of good fit make a clean break with conventional thinking on good governance. In fact, most current understandings of this agenda have not gone far enough. They have, as it were, paused en route at a dilapidated halfway house, from which they need to be evicted before they settle in for good. This halfway house has a technical name: it is called the principal–agent approach to public management reform (see Box 1.2). The road ahead, in contrast, involves the identification and solution of collective action problems.

We shall make clear what we mean by this, but it will help to begin by explaining one of the most prominent manifestations of the

---

Box 1.2 The principal–agent framework

A principal–agent problem exists where one party to a relationship (the principal) requires a service of another party (the agent) but the principal lacks the necessary information to monitor the agent's performance in an effective way (there is 'information asymmetry'). It is assumed here that the principal wants and requires the service, so that the difficulty to be overcome is distinctly about the agent's compliance with the principal's wishes and the information asymmetry that affects this.

---

central issue. This is the discussion of governance reform options in terms of a contrast between 'supply-side' approaches and 'demand-side' approaches.

For at least the past ten years, policy perspectives on improving governance in low-income countries have centred on a dialogue between so-called 'supply-side' and 'demand-side' approaches to governance reform. As will be seen, they are both versions of the good governance perspective. APPP research suggests that the demand/supply framework is a conceptual straitjacket and an obstacle to clear thinking about the challenges of African governance.

In the supply-side approach the implicit assumption is that governments are led by people whose central concern is to develop their countries. That is, they are genuinely, and without serious qualification, interested in effectively supplying the conditions for national development. They want governance and the economy to improve, with benefits for the population at large – this is their primary motivation. Therefore, donor-promoted reforms focus on how they can be assisted to supply the required changes and overcome the obstacles they face in meeting their objectives, especially by improving the functioning of public-sector institutions and the performance of public servants. Following the widespread failure of attempts to reform civil and public services directly by means of restructuring and training programmes, the favoured instruments of external support for the desired changes are budget support, technical assistance to public financial management and associated policy monitoring and dialogue.

In the 'demand-side' approach, the commitment of leaders to a development vision and to probity in public policy is acknowledged to be highly problematic in many instances – the primary political motivations are of other kinds. The supply-side approach to improving governance is criticised as managerialist and insufficiently sensitive to the political dimensions of the problem. It is argued that better governance and the effective provision of public goods are only likely when empowered citizens and mobilised civil societies begin to 'hold governments to account'. At this point, the implicit assumption is made that the citizens of poor countries have an uncomplicated desire and at least the potential ability to make demands on their rulers in their capacity as providers of public goods. External support is therefore directed towards the strengthening of specific 'vertical' and 'horizontal' accountability institutions and programmes to support citizen participation, 'voice' and empowerment, usually involving dissemination of information about rights and entitlements.

The dialogue between these twin perspectives has structured most thinking about both domestic reform options and aid delivery for the last fifteen years or so. It was in the mid-2000s that thinkers in and around the World Bank (World Bank 2003; Levy and Kpundeh 2004) began to argue, in the name of greater political realism, for a relative shift towards programmes that address the demand side of governance. An encompassing shift in the thinking of the development assistance community as a whole, including international and national NGOs, followed in short order and has been the dominant perspective ever since.

In terms of volume, it is no doubt true that the bulk of donor funding for governance reform has continued to flow through channels viewed by their critics as supply-oriented, including, notably, packages of budgetary aid or policy-based lending and public financial management reforms. On the other hand, it is probably accurate to say that the battle for intellectual supremacy has been won by advocates of demand-side work. The results have included extensive support to community monitoring of public services (through the use of 'score cards' for instance), programmes aimed at 'deepening democracy' and a variety of initiatives under the broad heading of 'social accountability'.

Most international development agencies still do a bit of both. Some are also making more deliberate efforts to link up what they do in the two areas. For example, they are earmarking a proportion of their budget-support spending to efforts to enhance domestic accountability, and encouraging more cross-departmental working between the teams managing budget-support operations and those working on citizen empowerment. To this extent, there is awareness that the 'either-supply-or-demand' structuring of governance-improvement options is unhelpful.

These bridging and rebalancing efforts do have a role to play. The 'silo working' that tends to characterise the departmental structures of development agencies is indeed an obstacle to effectiveness, and establishing more joined-up ways of working is a good first step. However, there is a more fundamental problem with the supply-versus-demand structuring of the options for governance improvement, one that is not so easily tackled and calls for a more radical solution.

This problem centres not on striking a better balance or generating more synergies but on something more basic. We need to revisit the assumptions both approaches make about the nature of African political reality. These assumptions produce analytical and policy weaknesses that mirror each other exactly. Since this has to do with the whole way the topic of governance for development is posed in Africa, it is an issue for domestic reformers and campaigners and not just for donors.

Throwing off the straitjacket of principal–agent thinking

The demand-side approach simply turns the supply-side approach on its head. The two perspectives share an important feature: an implicit assumption that there are sets of actors who are committed, in an uncomplicated way, to public-good objectives. They just differ about who those actors are: the supply-siders assume that national leaders are drivers of development, while demand-siders claim that it is more realistic to see the citizenry playing this role. In both approaches, the challenge of getting better governance is reduced to that of getting the other side to comply. Another way to put this is to say that both approaches are, in effect if not in intention, wedded to what is technically termed a 'principal–agent' model.

To avoid possible misunderstanding, the suggestion here is not that practitioners working on 'demand for good governance' use principal–agent concepts. Their typical watchwords are of course 'voice', 'empowerment' and 'accountability to citizens'. We also acknowledge that actual practice varies quite a lot, and sometimes involves many of the ingredients we promote in this book. On the other hand, what we sketch here and portray more fully below is very far from being our invention: it represents the dominant policy perspective for a large range of organisations which together exercise a massive influence on what happens on the ground in Africa.

Approaches that assume that either leaders or citizens in low-income countries have an uncomplicated commitment to improving governance and the provision of public goods are mistaken in roughly equal measure and for essentially the same reason. This is not to say there are no individuals who have a genuine interest in the development and transformation of their countries. But for practical purposes this is less important than the fact that most actors at all levels spend most of their time responding to relatively mundane concerns and that, when it comes to pursuing more ambitious objectives, they often face prohibitive problems of collective action.

Summarising in everyday terms, then, our position is that governance challenges in Africa are not fundamentally about one set of people getting another set of people to behave better in the interests of development. They are about both sets of people finding ways of being able to act collectively in their own and others' best interests. Reformers and development agencies have something useful to contribute to improving governance in Africa, but only if they appreciate that this is the fundamental nature of the challenge and other issues are secondary.

In slightly more technical terms, we are critical of approaches that conceptualise governance failings and remedies in terms that – whether they recognise it or not – adopt a principal–agent perspective. We believe it is more realistic to understand governance limitations as the product of multifaceted collective action problems, and to think about possible remedies on that basis. Principal–agent analysis still has some relevance to meeting development challenges, but it must be nested within an understanding of collective action challenges, not the other way round.

In articulating the APPP findings in this way, we have been inspired by the arguments developed with particular reference to the limitations of current anti-corruption programmes by Bo Rothstein and other members of the Quality of Government Institute at the University of Gothenburg (Persson et al. 2010; Rothstein 2011). They offer a key insight that has ramifications well beyond the particular field of anti-corruption (see Box 1.3). An underlying argument of the Gothenburg group, which we share, is that it is important not to make assumptions about what Africans want and will do, without reference to evidence and experience.

APPP findings agree with a good deal of other research and practical experience in suggesting that a realistic take on governance reform in Africa involves two things. First, it calls for an understanding of institutions and the underlying power relations that determine how they work in practice, and thus the nature of politics in the region. Secondly, it means appreciating that both elite incentives and the behaviour of citizens and service users are strongly affected by co-ordination and collective action challenges. Some of the challenges we are referring to are merely organisational, for which we reserve the term 'coordination'. The concept of collective action is used in a more technical sense, referring to the theory first elaborated by Olson (1965) and then developed by institutional theorists such as Hardin (1982), Sandler (1992) and particularly Ostrom (1990, 2005). This

---

Box 1.3 Collective action and anti-corruption

'… while contemporary anti-corruption reforms are based on a conceptualization of corruption as a principal–agent problem, in the African context corruption rather seems to resemble a collective action problem, making the short-term costs of fighting corruption outweigh the benefits. Consequently, even if most individuals morally disapprove of corruption and are fully aware of the negative consequences for the society at large, very few actors show a sustained willingness to fight it. This, in turn, leads to a breakdown of any anti-corruption reform that builds on the principal–agent framework … Insofar as a large enough number of actors are expected to play foul, everyone has something to gain personally from acting corruptly. Consequently, in a context in which corruption is the expected behavior … there will simply be no actors willing to take on the role of controlling corruption' (Persson et al. 2010: 1, 5).

theory is concerned with the particular conditions that, in a wide diversity of social settings, lead to the under-provision of public or collective goods (here in the narrower of the two senses distinguished in the Introduction).

As we explained briefly in the Introduction, public goods are technically defined as benefits (including services) that are consumed jointly by members of a given community. In other words, we are dealing with a situation in which one person's consumption of the benefit does not subtract from the availability of the good to others. More specifically, public goods are benefits from whose enjoyment it is impossible or difficult to exclude community members who have not contributed to their production. The classic instances extend from street lighting and unpolluted air to peace and security. The community in question can be anything from the families in a farming village, or the clients of a particular political patron, to the members of a country's political class.

The critical feature of the theory is the element of 'non-excludability'. This creates the so-called 'free-rider problem' (see Box 1.4), which leads to under-provision of the good. Common pool resources, such as shared forests and water systems, are distinguished from public goods proper by the fact that one person's use of the resource may well reduce its availability to others. However, non-excludability does apply. Because people who have contributed to the cost of the good are bound to share the benefits with a potentially large number of free-riders, their willingness to contribute will be undermined unless there are institutions (including forms of leadership) that limit such free-riding. The good will tend to be under-provided and, in the case of a common pool resource, may get overused, resulting in a 'tragedy of the commons'.

Box 1.4 The 'free-rider problem' explained

Free-riders are people who use more than their fair share of a resource and/or who cover less than their fair share of the costs of its production. This becomes a problem when it leads to the under-production of a public good or to the overuse of a common pool resource. Figuring out how to prevent or reduce free-riding is key to solving this problem.

As Ostrom and her school have shown, small-scale communities commonly do have institutions that prevent the destruction of common property or open-access resources such as forests or rivers. They can and do control free-riding. On the other hand, unresolved but potentially resolvable collective action problems are otherwise widespread and at the heart of the challenge of development (Gibson et al. 2005; Mockus 2005; Shivakumar 2005; Bano 2012). Those problems are, at least to some extent, subject to ameliorative action, but not so long as they are approached in a 'best practice' mode – where an internationally validated solution is applied without regard to the local context – or within a principal–agent perspective that assumes away the problems to be diagnosed and addressed.

It is important to appreciate the different policy and action implications of using a collective action framework rather than a principal–agent one. The latter approach assumes that there are principals that want goods to be provided or development to be promoted but have difficulty in getting the agents to perform and comply with their wishes because they lack relevant information. So the priority interventions are those enabling the collection and dissemination of information about entitlements and performance. Typical ways of doing this that have been enthusiastically adopted by the development business over the last decade have included systematic monitoring of policy implementation, public expenditure tracking surveys (PETS), community-level monitoring schemes using score cards and information campaigns focused on people's rights and entitlements. The fundamental idea is to mitigate the problem of information asymmetry, where agents have a great deal of information, especially about their own activities, and their principals have little.

Collective action theorists, on the other hand, are generally more sceptical about the motives that drive action. They are more keenly aware that many groups and individuals may want the benefits in the form of public or collective goods but will not work to obtain them, in part because of their expectations about the behaviour of others. Under these circumstances, providing them with better information with which to call others to account may be completely irrelevant. They will not be motivated to join with others to make use of this information, in part because they have other, easier and less risky ways of meeting their needs. For example, ordinary people may be linked to patrons who provide them with more reliable access to particular services, so they have little interest in contributing to public-wide efforts to improve provision. APPP research suggests that this situation is quite common, meaning that donor-funded interventions based on information-asymmetry assumptions have often been a waste of effort.

What's new and what isn't

There are two large problems with the way thinking about governance reform has been held within the straitjacket of principal–agent thinking. At the macro level, it tends to result in elite incentives getting treated as a 'black box' about which nothing further can be said, whereas there are at least a few important and policy-relevant things that can be said on the basis of research. At meso and micro levels, the assumption that ordinary people in poor developing countries can slip easily into the roles assigned to them by demand-side accountability initiatives leads to neglect of opportunities to diagnose and act upon collective action blockages.

As Kelsall (2013) has shown, when the black box of elite incentives is opened up it becomes clear that both historically and in the present there are important differences among political regimes in the way governance and development challenges are handled. In particular, the contrasts between the more and less developmental types of neopatrimonial politics are highly significant in shaping variations in outcomes. And these, in turn, are explained by whether or not the elites have been able to overcome the collective action problems they face in the pursuit of public policies that lead to sustained processes of economic transformation.

In the context of macro-political systems that are not geared to the provision of public goods, sectoral and sub-national actors face their own collective action problems. The macro constraints are often completely overwhelming. Occasionally, however, some immediate problems are able to be overcome despite the macro constraints, and these experiences are of special interest in thinking about reform and aid options for the future. In this book, we are concerned in a limited way and indirectly with macro-politics, because our examination of institutional blockages in public goods delivery leads us back to questions about political regimes, including the nature and limits of African democracy. More particularly, however, we are interested in unpacking the different ways in which local problem-solving occurs, and how it might be more often encouraged and less often undermined.

It should be clear that this is not just an APPP agenda. Most of our concerns are shared with other recent and several ongoing international research efforts, including the Developmental Leadership Program (Leftwich and Wheeler 2011; Wheeler and Leftwich 2012) and the Copenhagen-based Elites, Production and Poverty project (Whitfield and Therkildsen 2011). Some of the central themes of this book were incorporated in a Joint Statement on the political economy of African development issued by no fewer than five current research programmes in March 2012 (APPP et al. 2012).

Our work also builds on and adds to ten years of research at the Institute of Development Studies (Future State 2005, 2010; Citizenship DRC 2011). For example, one of the central conclusions from that research was that institutions that are successful in improving public services almost always involve actors on both sides of the divide between 'government' and 'citizens'. The boundaries between social mobilisation and political action are often blurred as well. We agree, and in this sense the ideas set out in this book are not new. On the other hand, we do not believe the lessons of the IDS research have been properly taken up. Such findings have often been translated into a simple message of the sort criticised above about joining up the demand and supply sides of governance reform. Our proposition is not about joining up demand and supply but about the prior question of how to address the severe problems of coordination and collective action that typically affect actors on both sides of the so-called demand–supply relationship.

This leads us to emphasise arrangements that assist problem-solving, as distinct from the single-stranded solutions or 'magic bullets' that have undue influence over development practice. Good institutions solve problems arising in *specific* circumstances, meaning that generic remedies will often miss the point and may well do harm. As we shall see, APPP research also suggests that the institutional arrangements that permit and/or consolidate successful problem-solving will often be hybrid arrangements that blend modern state principles and popular expectations or elements drawn from local cultures in a creative way. These propositions validate in a broad way the initial APPP 'hunch' about the value of 'working with the grain' of African societies. As the following chapters will show, however, this translates into two more specific and empirically testable claims:

- institutions that permit an adequate provision of public goods often do so by solving locally specific collective action problems; and
- hybrid forms are useful in this context as they reduce the costs of institutional innovation by combining modern professional standards or scientific criteria with local cultural borrowings.

The problem of magic bullets

Much of the preceding argument would be more easily accepted if it were not for the fact that most governance reform thinking is locked into one or other variant of the principal–agent approach. To give coherence to its own efforts, the development assistance business needs pithy, upbeat formulations that simplify complexity. It likes and needs panaceas, the silver bullets that can be counted upon to kill the evil-doer when all else has failed.

It is a familiar critique of the development enterprise that it is searching not for solutions to problems but for problems to which to attach known solutions. The more reflective practitioners often conclude that in particular fields 'the solution is the problem' (Pritchett and Woolcock 2008). As Olivier de Sardan (2012a) says on the basis of long experience in Niger, each one of a succession of modalities of provision, or modes of local governance, has been treated over time as *the* solution – the key that will open all doors. Following the first major setbacks to the bureaucratic efforts of the post-colonial state, there was a period in which 'participation' was the watchword and a variety of community-based committees and associations became the standard remedy. Privatisation of service provision, democratic decentralisation and even restoration of chiefly authority were each pursued with enthusiasm for a while. In reality, each of these modalities has had its serious problems and none has provided the expected miracle solution.

To the extent that there are solutions, they are to be found in the fine detail of implementation, within and across the modalities. As argued by Olivier de Sardan (2012b: 9–12), enlightened reformers exist, to some degree, within each mode of local governance, and progress is more likely to be made by providing new opportunities to such people than by treating any one approach as intrinsically superior. Later in the book, we flesh out this idea – an idea that rests on a radical interpretation of the 'good fit' approach and, therefore, what it means to anchor institutions in country realities. Here we discuss further three magic bullets or panaceas that remain influential or are still in the ascendant today: democratic decentralisation, client power and social accountability. Each may be considered to be rooted in the good-governance framework and each makes behavioural assumptions of the principal–agent type.

Democratic decentralisation Devolution of power to elected district or municipal governments is often seen as the best way of addressing obstacles to public goods provision. Properly implemented, democratic decentralisation or a municipal mode of local governance is held to be *the* solution to the problem of persistent poverty. The principal obstacle is seen as the unwillingness of central governments to implement the measure properly, by actually conceding decision-making powers and providing the necessary resources to local actors.

Devolution of resources and decisions to elected local governments has been advocated on various grounds, some of them quite technical and carefully qualified (e.g. World Bank 1997: ch. 7). Such devolution has been implemented by governments for different reasons, most of them highly political.[1] However, the most common argument among bilateral donors and NGOs starts from the assumption that the demand expressed for public goods by service users and the general population is an important influence on their provision. It then asserts that the physical distance separating the provider from the user affects the strength and effectiveness of user 'voice' and hence the provider response. Putting the argument more technically, the provision of public goods is a principal–agent challenge, where the principal is the client or service user, and the local authorities and service providers are their agents. It is suggested that the information asymmetry and the 'agency loss' (non-compliance) that affect principal–agent relationships in general are likely to be reduced by the factor of proximity.

There is in fact no body of theory underpinning this claim that democratic decentralisation obviously favours the provision of public goods.[2] Democratic decentralisation may be intrinsically desirable, but Treisman's (2007) critique of the theoretical foundations of the

---

1 See, for example, Blundo (1998), Andersson et al. (2004), Cammack et al. (2007), Eaton et al. (2010) and Poteete and Ribot (2011).

2 Other than the literature on fiscal federalism, and that deals with a different set of issues.

decentralisation movement is comprehensive. He finds no valid theoretical argument for expecting decentralised governance to be more or less effective than a centralised system in terms of public goods performance. Two criticisms can be made of the assumption that decentralisation promotes public goods delivery. First, public goods provision is only partly about services for which there is 'demand' and about which, to any degree, it is sensible to see local populations as clients or principals. Secondly, where the principal–agent concept may apply, the importance of physical distance on its own is highly questionable (World Bank 2003: ch. 10; Golooba-Mutebi 2005).

As for empirical research, it too points in a different direction. At the end of the first decade of intensive decentralising reforms, Richard Crook and associates (Crook and Manor 1998; Crook and Sverrisson 2003) concluded that the impacts of democratic decentralisation on outcomes such as the effectiveness of poverty-reduction efforts are indeterminate. That is, the outcomes depend heavily on factors other than the decision to devolve powers and resources to lower levels of public authority. The context, including the political complexion of the central government and the interest that the regime or other forces have in capturing local power for their purposes, makes a vast difference. The bulk of the ever-expanding literature on decentralisation continues to be clear on this: the 'other' factors are crucial.[3]

The obvious implication is that the focus for policy research should be on the nature of these 'other' factors. This has been followed up in one sense, with studies increasingly starting from what it takes to get better public services and working backwards to evaluate a large range of delivery institutions, as in the 2004 World Development Report, *Making Services Work for Poor People* (World Bank 2003).

This shift on the part of thinkers has, however, had little impact on the way decentralisation is promoted at country level and campaigned for at the global level. Democratic decentralisation has certainly lost some of its allure in international circles, partly because of the lack of decisive empirical support and positive outcomes. Nonetheless, significant vested interests, not least within African countries, continue to advocate for district and municipal government. In this context, bold claims continue to be made – and gain credibility by repetition

---

3 See, among others, Smoke (2003), Ndegwa and Levy (2004), Ahmad et al. (2005), Bardhan (2005), Jütting et al. (2005), Olowu (2006), Crawford and Hartmann (2008), Saito (2008), ARD Inc. (2010) and Connerley et al. (2010).

– that local government has a 'comparative advantage', or at least a 'potential comparative advantage', in essential service provision. This, it is argued, is because of the 'potentially greater pressure for responsiveness and accountability on local development decision-making' or because '[l]ocal governments' proximity to the people they are intended to serve fosters accountability, better governance and democratic learning' (Bonfiglio 2003: 68; Global Forum on Local Development 2010: 4, 7).

This is unfortunate. According to the view we take in this book, both the local anchorage of governance arrangements and the scope for local problem-solving are vital issues. However, they are not the same as decentralisation and suffer by association with this agenda. In short, the conventional case for decentralisation has become a source of 'noise' that is unhelpful to the case for more genuine localisation.

Rediscovering 'demand': client power Despite the important advances it marked, the above-mentioned 2004 World Development Report (WDR) has itself become a source of magic-bullet thinking. Along with other World Bank publications (Levy and Kpundeh 2004), it inaugurated a period during which all the innovative thinking about the governance of public services has been about 'demand'. Considerable Bank lending and other donor funding have continued to go into so-called supply-side reforms, notably in the form of budget support and technical assistance to public sector management (despite very mixed evaluation evidence on their effectiveness). However, the exciting stuff has been about finding new and better ways to stimulate the demand for better governance-for-development.

The 2004 WDR is a finely documented study in which there is much that is still of interest. However, it was also the fulcrum upon which the aid business turned on the issue of supply-versus-demand approaches to the governance of service provision. It was the influential proponent of an elementary non sequitur: aid needs to become more politically attuned; therefore, it needs to focus on stimulating citizen demand for services and accountability. Since 2004, political governance programming has become almost synonymous with voice, transparency and accountability projects and other demand-side interventions.

Like Levy and Kpundeh (ibid.), the 2004 WDR began with an argument for moving from managerial to institutional reforms. It offered path-breaking flashes of political realism, for example: 'Politicians often use the control of publicly provided services as a mechanism of clientelism – for both citizens and providers. ... Services are allocated in ways that reward (or punish) communities for their political support. Sometimes the ministry is the servant of the providers, not the other way around, and providers capture the policymaking' (World Bank 2003: 51–2).

However, this recognition of the lack of political interest in providing quality public services was not followed up. Nor were the reasons for weak citizen control over politicians examined further. Focused attention was given instead to the difficulties that an assumed governmental 'principal' has in getting service providers (its 'agents') to be performance-oriented. Since this and previous work in the same vein (e.g. Leonard 2000) led to doubts about the feasibility of monitoring providers effectively, the authors changed tack. They questioned the viability of the so-called 'long route of accountability' – i.e. boosting accountability of providers to citizens/clients via policy-makers and politicians – and promoted the so-called 'short route of accountability', which became the main policy innovation with which the WDR has been associated since.

This new policy included a range of devices to make providers accountable *directly* to clients by mobilising client and citizen 'demand' for better provision. Various examples were set out which, it was argued, support the feasibility of short-route successes on a significant scale. All involved stimulating demand and empowering citizens by providing them with information. In the field, this often took the form of local 'consciousness-raising' initiatives and 'civil society strengthening' targeted at NGOs specialising in community empowerment.

The weakness in this thinking is that the flash of political realism that was used to shed doubt on the original supply-side version of the principal–agent story is not applied to the demand side. The political, social and organisational limitations that ordinary Africans face as principals 'demanding' better public services or more responsible governance are passed over very lightly. Discussion of these limitations is not entirely absent from the texts, but they are not given significant weight.

In our view, the results to be obtained from client empowerment through the promotion of information dissemination and government transparency have been seriously oversold in the years since 2004 on the basis of a partial reading of key bits of evidence. The selective dissemination of WDR 2004 led into a wider problem of selective reading of studies and reports for the sake of agencies sustaining some simple, upbeat message about the potential of 'bottom-up' initiatives.

There are several well-worn examples. One is the Bangalore citizens' score-cards experiment, which has been widely copied across the world, including in Africa. Others concern the claimed impact of publishing budget information on school funding in Uganda, and later work on community monitoring of health services in Uganda. A typical fault in the reporting of evidence – one that is not necessarily reduced by the use of advanced statistical techniques – is that an incomplete account is given of the importance of the contextual factors that contributed to the success of the highlighted intervention. It is clear enough in the detailed descriptions of the experiments that top-down performance pressures and/or activities that affected provider incentives made important contributions to the recorded outcomes. Yet the role of these factors disappears from view when the results are summarised and disseminated. We have developed this criticism in the necessary detail in other published work (Booth 2012b). Suffice it to say here that because contextual factors are vital to success, single-stranded summaries of how such interventions 'worked' are liable to be misleading and a bad basis for attempts at replication.

Social accountability Social accountability (Malena et al. 2004) is undoubtedly the most engaging of the current mantras of the development business. A good deal of serious development work is being done under this heading, usually by local and international NGOs with official donor support. The flow of interesting writing on the subject seems set to continue. Unfortunately, however, the magic-bullet mind-set is alive and well in this field too. Social accountability is promoted as one single thing with well-understood common features. In the predominant discourse, the richness of the actual experience of working with citizen groups on public goods issues is reduced to a depoliticised 'widget' or mechanism (Joshi and Houtzager 2012).

Once again, the common feature for development success is assumed to be the mobilisation of citizen demand for accountability – citizens as principals, with national and local politicians and bureaucrats as their agents. The entry point is the enhancement of information supply, transparency and awareness of rights delivered to civil-society organisations or social movements.

The field of social accountability has been the subject of good previous critiques. The burden of this research is that client 'voice' is a weak source of accountability for performance unless accompanied by strong top-down pressures of some kind. What works to improve public service provision is an effective combination of initiatives that change behaviour among both suppliers and users.[4] According to the Future State Centre (2010), success has been achieved in various parts of the world, notably in Latin America, where all or most of the following elements have come together:

- emergence of a political leadership with an enhanced interest in winning elections on a public goods basis;
- interest within the professional organisations of providers in improving their public reputation;
- linkage of social movements to political parties; and
- client and voter interest in improved performance.

This is the complex combination that sometimes works. The Future State authors are explicit about two things. First, while not all the elements may be necessary, some sort of change in incentives and action on the provider side seems essential if user or voter pressure is to have any significant effects. Secondly, the whole process needs to be political. In this, they are supported by the Citizenship DRC's *Blurring the Boundaries* (2011), which quotes Gaventa and McGee (2010: 34): 'Competition for formal political power is also central, creating new impetus for reform, and bringing key allies into positions of influence, often in synergy with collective action from below.' In short, 'social' accountability is a misnomer – this is politics! What we would further suggest is that within each of the categories of actors that contributed to these processes – politicians, leaders of parties, trade unions and social movements, and service-user groups – special efforts were no doubt needed to convince individuals to engage in what would have been a probably unprecedented level of constructive collective action.

---

4 See Goetz et al. (2001), Future State (2005: ch. 3), Joshi (2007), O'Neil et al. (2007), Houtzager et al. (2008), Rocha Menocal and Sharma (2008), Future State (2010: ch. 4), Gaventa and McGee (2010), McGee and Gaventa (2010) and Citizenship DRC (2011).

What the research findings add up to, then, is that it is a serious mistake to treat citizens and service users as 'principals' with an uncomplicated interest in better governance and better public services. Although they are victims, they have options, most of which are less costly, less risky and more likely to yield the desired result than organising to demand improvement from an unresponsive state. In this sense, they are far more complicit in current patterns of bad governance than the principal–agent framework would imply. They are complicit despite the fact that they are victims. On the other hand, service delivery personnel are themselves, often enough, victims of the poor management and unreliable resourcing of public provision. In both cases, the disjunction between pursuing current interests and real, long-term interests happens because individuals and groups face collective action problems.

By any standards, this is a telling body of evidence against the simple idea of building the demand side to achieve development, an idea that has steered governance work by official donors and international and local NGOs over the past decade. There are signs that it has put a serious dent in the orthodoxy. The latest evidence summaries from World Bank researchers acknowledge not only that the big remaining question is about the incentives of higher-level leadership, but that 'the most important domain for greater accountability is via power and politics'. They also admit that 'generalized, "best practice" initiatives for greater civil society engagement are likely to fail' (Devarajan et al. 2011: abstract, 34). In belated recognition of positions advanced a decade earlier (e.g. Brett 2003), a comprehensive review of previous World Bank initiatives in 'participatory development' has now been published (Mansuri and Rao 2012). It provides a systematic, evidence-based critique of approaches that treat induced community participation as a substitute for forceful action on the part of the state.

In practice, some donor-funded technical assistance staff and NGOs actually engage in the facilitation of collective action solutions in ways that cut across the divide between providers and clients, or officials and private citizens. Sometimes they do this in the context of projects that are formally committed to one of the above-named magic bullets – 'demanding accountability', citizen score cards, etc. There is no doubt, however, that their formal adherence to these tricks of the good-governance agenda hinders the context-sensitive work they are doing. No less important, it prevents the accumulation of a reliable evidence base on what they have achieved and why they achieved it. If our argument is correct, it is time for greater consistency between what these projects are actually doing and the 'theory of change' to which they are formally committed. Development organisations that have already moved on from a principal–agent diagnosis to creating space for local problem-solving and facilitating collective action should come out of the closet and say so!

Until this happens, we must expect a continuing flow of publications and blogs documenting social accountability initiatives in Africa and worldwide for largely promotional purposes (Odugbemi and Jacobson 2008; McNeil and Malena 2010). Without analysing other contextual drivers of change, large claims are made in this literature about the potential of citizen demand and social movements, or about the mobilising power of information. Practical 'lessons' are drawn. However, generating evidence on effectiveness has not been a priority, and this has not stopped the World Bank from launching, as recently as 2012, a new Global Partnership for Social Accountability, a mechanism to support beneficiary groups and civil society organisations operating on the demand side of service provision (World Bank 2012).

One of the reasons for this inconsistency between practice and theory is undoubtedly the lack of an obvious alternative panacea for poor governance and low-quality public goods provision. This book does not aim to provide one. However, we agree with Merilee Grindle (2011) that researchers have a duty to provide more than negative messages and evidence of complexity. There needs to be a meeting point between researchers' recognition of complexity and practitioners' hunger for guidance. That meeting point is what we would call middle-range theory. This book has such a theory. It is about the centrality of collective action problems in governance for development in Africa.

Summing up

We began this chapter with the growing expert consensus on the bankruptcy of a 'best practice' concept of governance improvement in Africa, and the need for this consensus to become more specific about the likely content of the alterative 'good fit' approach. The specific content we propose involves giving a more central place to the identification and resolution of collective action problems at the many levels where 'governance' is a problem for development.

We then argued that an obstacle to this realistic agenda is the fact that current policy responses rely heavily on a series of questionable magic bullets or cure-all remedies. Those that have remained prominent during the last decade – democratic decentralisation, client power and social accountability – rest on assumptions about good governance and about citizen 'demand' that are empirically and theoretically questionable. They assume implicitly that ordinary citizens stand in a principal–agent relationship to governments and service providers, whereas the research evidence suggests that ordinary citizens face collective action problems, as do politicians and providers, and that the solutions that are sometimes found are both highly interactive and highly political.

2 | THE COUNTRY CONTEXTS

This book offers an alternative vision of governance for development which we think is widely applicable across low-income sub-Saharan Africa. It draws on a body of research covering a total of eighteen countries, parts of which have been more fully reflected in the recent Zed Books title by Kelsall (2013). The present book is based primarily on fieldwork undertaken in four countries, in each of which teams of fieldworkers and research leaders spent periods of many months in selected locations. In this chapter we provide a little background on these four countries and some details on the site selection and on the fieldwork approach. We also indicate the additional research that we draw on most directly.

Some common features and basic concepts

The four countries where the bulk of the APPP Local Governance fieldwork was carried out – Malawi, Niger, Rwanda and Uganda – are all low-income countries of small- to medium-sized population. They share a number of other features. They are all landlocked and located within sub-Saharan Africa's tropical belt. With some exceptions, noted below, they are little endowed with non-agricultural and non-pastoral natural resources. All have been affected by being in conflictive neighbourhoods and, with the exception of Malawi, they have experienced internal wars within the last generation. Their people qualify therefore on several counts as members of Paul Collier's (2007) 'bottom billion' of the population of the globe.

Underlying the significant differences that come into focus below and in later chapters, there are also commonalities in terms of fundamental economic and political structures. All four economies have small formal sectors. Most economic actors are households. There are few fully capitalist firms and fewer still that are productive rather than commercial enterprises. Competitive markets are weakly developed. The social class structure is therefore non-capitalist, or not-yet-capitalist. For closely related reasons, political systems allow only limited forms of civil and popular participation. All of the countries are nominally democratic – with regular elections, presidents and parliaments, independent judiciaries and relatively free expression. However, these institutions usually do not function in the same way as in advanced capitalist democracies.

There are several ways of characterising such a state of affairs using social science concepts. One that emphasises particularly the interdependencies between the level of development of capitalist socio-economic relations and the type of politics that is possible is the concept of 'limited access order' (LAO) elaborated by North et al. (2009, 2013). In an LAO, both access to markets and access to politics are restricted by comparison with the 'open access orders' that have come to prevail during the last century in the global North.

A related concept is neopatrimonialism. Unfortunately, this term has come to be widely used as a term of abuse, closely related to 'corruption', and the misleading impression has been given that it describes a specifically African cultural tendency. We use it in the classical sense, where it arises from Max Weber's (1978 [1922]) studies of early modern Europe and Asia. In this usage, patrimonial systems are those in which there is little or no distinction between the ruler's household and the affairs of the state. The officials in patrimonial systems are distinguished from those in modern bureaucracies by a lack of separation between their 'private' and 'official' spheres of activity (ibid.: 1028). The addition of the prefix 'neo' signals that the system in question is governed by some sort of hybrid of patrimonial and what Weber called rational-legal principles of legitimacy and rules of conduct. The best treatment of the topic is in van de Walle (2001). Countries that are LAOs in the terms used by North et al. are likely also to have neopatrimonial systems as discussed by van de Walle. These concepts are essential in coming to grips with the country realities of Malawi, Niger, Rwanda and Uganda.

We do not elaborate further here because one of the themes of this book, as well as of Kelsall (2013), is that the differences *among* neopatrimonial systems (and LAOs) have been under-emphasised in policy debates about Africa. However, in Chapter 4 we review features of the average or modal type of African neopatrimonial system in connection with the effects of democratic politics on the management of development in Malawi, Niger and Uganda.

Malawi

Malawi occupies 94,000 square kilometres of land area along the western shores of the southernmost of Africa's Great Lakes. It borders Tanzania in the north, Zambia in the west and Mozambique in the south, and was home to 15 million people in 2010.[1] Its economy remains largely agricultural and is dependent on a single rainy season. Commercial life is centred in one major city, Blantyre. While urbanisation is rapid, only about 20% of the population lives in towns. The last estimate placed 74% of the population under the international PPP $1.25 a day poverty line, down from 83% in the late 1990s. Life expectancy at birth was fifty-two years for men and fifty-four years for women in 2008.

After its independence from Britain in 1964, Malawi was ruled by the autocrat Hastings Kamuzu Banda for thirty years before the democratic transition of 1994 saw the inception of a multi-party political system. The new government was led by President Bakili Muluzi. As it turned out this was a 'transition without transformation', as many of the ills that afflicted political and economic development at the end of Banda's dictatorship have persisted. Some in fact were made worse by the transition.

Many Malawians speak about their society as now having 'too much freedom'. What they mean is that the rules and regulations that Kamuzu Banda enforced – and which ensured that basic public services were delivered – have come to be enforced with unwelcome laxity. Politics under Banda was of the patron–client sort, but now clientelism is overlaid with the effects of vigorous multi-party competition, regular elections and improved though fluctuating respect for civil rights. At times, the results have been a corruption 'free for all', with leaders using state resources with impunity to promote their parties and their political and personal fortunes. What remained of Kamuzu Banda's merit-based civil service has been undermined by political patronage and weak rule enforcement. Presidential power has been used systematically to buy political loyalty, substantially reducing the effectiveness of constitutional checks and balances.

In 2004, after two presidential terms characterised by macro-economic chaos and political turmoil (including an unsuccessful bid

---

1 Unless otherwise indicated, economic and population data in this chapter are from the World Bank's World Development Indicators.

for a third term), Bakili Muluzi promoted Bingu wa Mutharika's candidacy as president. They fell out soon after Mutharika came to power, however, and the new president was incentivised to build support for himself and his new party (the DPP) by fostering economic growth. This he did with some success. But the president's bid in his second term to ensure that his brother Peter Mutharika succeeded him as president in 2014 led him into serious mismanagement of the economy and an increasingly authoritarian style of rule. His unexpected death in April 2012 saw his vice-president, Joyce Banda, take over. With a small political-party base, she has been governing by building a new coalition aimed at delivering an economic turnaround.

Malawi remains one of the poorest and least developed countries in Africa. Its development policies have been largely donor driven, although Mutharika sought to reduce the influence of foreigners. Few of the elite understand the need for economic transformation and most political leaders are more concerned with their own careers than with national development.

The state is generally weak and largely absent from the peri-urban areas where APPP research on the delivery of four public goods was undertaken. In 2009/10, seventeen weeks' research was carried out among 'translocal' populations – people whose livelihood strategies depend on both the urban economy and their rural landholdings – in Rumphi, Kasungu and Blantyre. A further ten months of participatory observation was undertaken in Ndirande township in Blantyre in 2010/11. In parallel, further investigations on governance and public goods were undertaken in Lilongwe, Chiradzulu, Rumphi, Kasungu and Zomba towns.

Decentralised governance structures and systems exist in law but are only partially implemented. Chieftaincy remains important, even in Ndirande, the large informal settlement in the city of Blantyre where more than a half-million people live (UN-Habitat 2011). In towns, traditional leaders and some newly selected block leaders (also popularly called chiefs, *mfumu*) fill the gaps left by local government and help people access public services. One legacy of thirty years of single-party rule is that party-political structures and leaders remain influential right down to the local level. Governance issues such as these heavily influence the way in which the four public goods under study are delivered to peri-urban residents.

Niger

Niger occupies a vast land area (1,267,000 square kilometres) and had 15.5 million inhabitants in 2010. It is located in the Sahel region of north-west Africa, bordered by Algeria and Libya to the north, Mali and Burkina Faso to the West, Benin and Nigeria to the south and Chad to the west. The country is an important source of uranium but otherwise the economy is largely agricultural and pastoral. The only major city is the capital, Niamey. The latest estimate placed 66% of the population under the international PPP $1.25 a day poverty line, compared with 78% in 1994. Life expectancy at birth was fifty-one years for men and fifty-two years for women in 2008.

Niger became independent of France in 1960 but remained in the French Community. Since then its transition from colonialism to democratic rule has been pushed off course repeatedly by single-party authoritarianism, insurgencies in the north and military coups. Tensions between autocratic state-centrism – including administrative chiefdom (canton chiefs, group chiefs, tribal chiefs and village chiefs until 2004) – and more participatory forms of governance were evident throughout the period.

New factors affecting governance emerged in the 1990s. They included structural adjustment, begun a few years earlier; years of unpaid salaries; the rolling back of the state from certain of its service functions and areas of authority; and the coming of multi-partyism and electoral patronage. Secondary effects include a generalisation of corruption; a real freedom of expression and the press (despite a few hitches); greater and greater dependence on external aid; and the increasingly visible presence of projects and NGOs in the local landscape. Two outstanding characteristics of recent decades have been conversion of the political and state elite to an unbridled form of competitive political patronage, fuelled by a growing involvement of big traders and other business interests, and an increased dependence on aid.

In 1999 Tandja Mamadou was elected president and, in July 2004, municipal elections were held as part of the nation's first decentralisation process. Over 3,500 representatives – councillors and mayors – were elected to new local governments in 265 newly established *communes* (municipalities). Tandja Mamadou was re-elected president at the end of the year in what were deemed relatively free and fair elections. But insecurity emerging from a second Tuareg revolt decimated the economy, and the president sought to hold on to power for a third term. This was met by political unrest in 2009 and a coup by the military, who promised a return to civilian rule. This promise was kept. Parliamentary elections were held and Mahamadou Issoufou was elected president in early 2011.

APPP research into the local governance of public goods provision was undertaken between 2009 and 2011 at three sites – Balleyara (in Dosso region), Say (in Tillabéri region) and Guidan Roumji (in Maradi region). Five field researchers from LASDEL worked in these three urban/rural municipalities for a month in 2009 and for several weeks in 2010. These small towns were selected as municipal headquarters hosting significant public services, some economic infrastructure and a variety of forms of governance. They each offered a distinct set of sociocultural and linguistic characteristics.

Balleyara is a town of Touareg population, but of Zarma language, dominated by market gardening and an international market. Say is a town of Peul (Fulani) population, and of Peul (Fulani) and Zarma language, on the banks of a river where people undertake fishing and mixed agro-pastoral activities. Guidan Roumdji is a Hausa-speaking town of Gobirawa population, on the main national road and close to Nigeria, with trade and agricultural production on a considerable scale.

These sites offered the advantage that the fieldworkers knew the areas in some depth from previous research and were able to draw on existing knowledge and contacts. Several of the LASDEL fieldworkers were in addition able to draw on experience of studying local administration and public goods provision in many other parts of Niger over a much longer period (Olivier de Sardan et al. 2010a).

Rwanda

Rwanda is the most compact country of our set, occupying just 24,670 square kilometres of land area and accommodating a population of 11 million in 2010. It is located between Uganda and Tanzania to the north and west, Burundi to the south and the Democratic Republic of Congo to the west. Its economy remains overwhelmingly agricultural, with commercial life centred in the capital, Kigali. The poverty headcount using the international PPP $1.25 a day poverty line was 63% in 2011, down from 77% in 2000. Life expectancy at birth was forty-eight years for men and fifty-two years for women in 2008.

Rwanda's violent modern history began in the period 1959–62

when the departing Belgians transferred power to the leaders of the Hutu majority rather than to the Tutsis through whom they had ruled until then. Two Hutu-led regimes headed by Presidents Grégoire Kayibanda (1961–73) and Juvenal Habyarimana (1973–94) placed restrictions on Tutsis in the name of Hutu social liberation. These measures and intermittent outbreaks of mass killing generated large refugee communities on the country's borders, especially in Uganda and DRC, both of which had large Rwandaphone populations of their own. Otherwise, the pre-1994 governments followed the trends of their time, adopting single-party rule and aid-funded development efforts. Habyarimana's government was influenced somewhat by the Tanzanian model of African socialism and was well regarded by development agencies until a severe economic recession began to affect the country in the late 1980s.

The economic downturn coincided with the invasion from Uganda by the forces of the Rwandan Patriotic Front (RPF) and with the conversion of the international community to the virtues of competitive multi-party politics. Notoriously, genocidal killings ensued in 1994 as the world stood by. The RPF's military victory brought in a new regime within months, and by 2000 this was consolidated in very much the form it assumes today, with Paul Kagame as president and the RPF party providing a strong steer to a governing coalition including several much smaller parties.

Under Kagame, Rwandan governments have been widely criticised for restricting political competition, disallowing parties with any affinities with the former Hutu radicals and imposing their high-minded vision for the country on a relatively passive national population. Their military exploits in the DRC during the wars of 1996–2002 won them grudging admiration but few friends. They have, however, been equally applauded, sometimes prematurely, for bringing about a sustained economic recovery, high economic growth rates and, especially within the last five years, notable improvements in social indicators. Rwanda has always had a reputation for state efficiency, and some of this may be due to the fact that, unlike most states in Africa, the country has a long history as a political entity. However, observers attribute the RPF's commitment to national development, and the determination and intelligence it devotes to implementing its policies, to the shock of the genocide and the enduring threat represented by armed groups descended from the *génocidaires* in the forests of the DRC.

Some of Rwanda's recent successes have seemed too striking to be believable. 'Is the bride too beautiful?' APPP researchers from other country teams enquired. As our discussion in Chapter 3 makes clear, we do not think the differences in development outcomes between Rwanda and the other three countries are so large as to stretch credibility, and the chains of causation are quite apparent and straightforward.

In Rwanda fieldwork was undertaken in Nyamagabe and Musanze districts, which are located in the southern and northern provinces respectively. We do not claim that these are 'typical' Rwandan districts. APPP research was geared to discovering 'what works' in the governance of public goods provision. In both Rwanda and Uganda, therefore, research sites were selected with a view to uncovering causes of progress, rather than adding to the literature of failure. That said, both districts have had difficult histories from the point of view of the RPF government and were not in that sense likely showcases.

Nyamagabe had been one of Rwanda's most underdeveloped regions and the site of severe food crises as recently as the mid-2000s. At the end of the genocide, it was within the area occupied by French troops under Operation Turquoise rather than by the RPF forces. Musanze, part of the former Ruhengeri District, had had close ties to former President Habyarimana and his MRND party, and was the location of the most serious anti-RPF insurgency after 1994.

Research was done in three 'sectors' (sub-district units) of Nyamagabe: Cyanika, which is located 5 kilometres from the district headquarters, and Kaduha and Musange, which are both more remote. In Musanze District two sectors were selected: Kinigi, on the edge of the Virunga mountains and the National Park, and Gacaca sector in the district's mountainous lake region. The field team spent a total of eleven months living in or close to the research sites between November 2009 and March 2011.

Uganda

Uganda is the largest of our four study countries in population terms (33.4 million in 2010) and occupies a land area about twice that of Malawi (200,000 square kilometres). It is located in east Africa, inland from Kenya, with Tanzania and Rwanda to the south, the Democratic Republic of Congo to the west and South Sudan to the north. It has a relatively diversified economy, with coffee and other significant export sectors. Industrial and service activities are increasingly significant, mostly located in the capital, Kampala. Fifty-one per cent of the population was living under the international PPP $1.25 a day poverty line in 2005, as compared with 57% in 2002. Life expectancy at birth was fifty-two years for men and fifty-three years for women in 2008.

As in Rwanda, the current political leadership emerged from an internal war. President Yoweri Museveni has been in office since he seized power at the end of an extended guerrilla conflict in 1986. In his first phase of rule, he presided over a 'no-party' system in which his National Resistance Movement (NRM) claimed to incorporate all the country's political tendencies and ethnic identities and to a limited extent did so. The credibility of these claims was progressively undermined, especially after opposition groups within the NRM began to break ranks and contest elections. Since 2005, Uganda has had a formal multi-party constitution, and Museveni has retained power following strongly contested elections.

He has done so on the basis of politically astute measures of presidential patronage blended with substantial doses of electoral intimidation. The NRM party is much more of a personal vehicle than Rwanda's RPF. However, as in Rwanda, political stability depends quite heavily on the links between the president's party and the army, with the mass of rural voters tending to support the incumbents as the guarantors of continued peace.

For many years, Uganda was considered a development success story and a donor darling because economic growth was rapid and poverty rates declined sharply. Much of this success was due, however, to a single, wise policy measure, the liberalisation of coffee marketing, which spread the gains from structural adjustment measures widely and deeply. Uganda was also an early exponent of democratic decentralisation and has been the site of a great many experiments in community participation in social infrastructure investment and public service delivery. Especially since the advent of formal multi-partyism, however, the creation of new districts has become an important instrument of political patronage for the president and these and decisions on local taxation and user charges have severely weakened previously functioning delivery systems.

A first phase of research was undertaken for APPP by a team managed by the Kampala-based Development Research and Training

(DRT). This lasted for three months and covered a regionally diverse set of research sites in Ntungamo District (south-west Uganda), Kumi District (eastern Uganda) and Masaka and Rakai Districts (central Uganda). For the subsequent, more extended, fieldwork, Masaka and Rakai were selected on the basis that APPP was interested in the drivers of success as well as failure. According to official statistics, the two districts were relatively good performers in public service provision. It was assumed that this was due in part to their location in the relatively accessible and politically well-represented central/ south-west region.

Masaka and Rakai are contiguous – united as one district previously – and both were part of the former Buganda kingdom. Of the two, Rakai has fewer natural wetlands, leading to water shortages during the dry season. It was the epicentre of an HIV/AIDS epidemic, which devastated its human resource base. Masaka District includes the town of Masaka, a major centre on the road leading to the Rwandan border. Although the kingdoms of western Uganda exist formally only for 'cultural' purposes, traditional leaders owing loyalty to the Kabaka (the Buganda king) remain influential in the two districts. Whether or not this factor played any continuing role in public goods provision was of interest to the research team, although findings on this subject were rather inconclusive.

In Masaka, two sub-counties called Lwabenge and Buwunga were selected for fieldwork. In Rakai, Kabira and Dwaniro sub-counties were selected. In each sub-county, two villages were studied in depth, the field teams spending most of the twelve months from May 2010 to April 2011 in these sites, with short breaks and supervisory visits from research coordinators at regular intervals.

Other study countries

The other countries where individual research (by PhD candidates) was completed in time to contribute to the APPP Local Governance findings were Senegal, Sierra Leone and Tanzania. In this book we also draw on the APPP research into Business and Politics, Local Justice, Parental Preferences and Religious Education, and State Bureaucracies. These streams of work brought into the picture perspectives from DRC, Ghana, Kenya, Mali and Senegal among others, as well as additional material on Niger, Rwanda, Malawi and Tanzania.

3 | MATERNAL HEALTH: WHY IS RWANDA DOING BETTER THAN MALAWI, NIGER AND UGANDA?

So far, we have outlined the argument of the book and introduced the countries in which we undertook the major fieldwork. Now we begin to show how research into public goods provision led us towards the view that governance challenges in Africa are more about collective action problems than about principal–agent relationships. Our starting point is one of the four areas of provision selected for study across the countries: safe motherhood or maternal health.

Safe motherhood is a key objective for all developing countries, and reducing maternal mortality worldwide by three-quarters is Millennium Development Goal number 5. In most countries progress is being made, but sub-Saharan Africa remains the most dangerous region of the world in which to give birth. It is also the case that the rate of progress among African countries and in different time periods is variable. Rwanda's recent performance in this field has been notably better than that of the other three countries in our set, and this chapter explains why.

The analysis proceeds in steps. First we discuss typical bottlenecks in provision and the extent to which they were apparent in our research sites and across the four countries. Then we advance the hypothesis that the significant differences are largely explained by the presence or absence of three types of institutional blockage. Importantly, these do not include the kinds of factors emphasised in mainstream thinking about good governance, democratic decentralisation, client power or social accountability. Finally, we ask why these blockages are less apparent in Rwanda than in the other countries, the answer to which supports our contention that development challenges are fundamentally problems of collective action.

The problem

Maternal mortality is defined as the 'death of a woman while pregnant or within 42 days of termination of pregnancy, irrespective of the duration and site of the pregnancy, from any cause related to or aggravated by the pregnancy or its management but not from accidental or incidental causes' (WHO n.d.). Despite recent progress, access to appropriate health-care remains inadequate, meaning that many women still do not survive pregnancy and childbirth. This is most striking in sub-Saharan Africa, where the overwhelming majority of the world's maternal deaths take place. Sub-Saharan Africa experienced an average maternal mortality ratio (MMR) of 500 per 100,000 live births in 2010, anything over 300 being considered 'high' (UNFPA 2012).

Main causes of maternal death There is consensus that most of the main causes of death during and following pregnancy and childbirth – severe bleeding (post-partum haemorrhage), infections (sepsis), high blood pressure, obstructed labour and unsafe abortions – are preventable or manageable (WHO 2004). Antenatal care during pregnancy and the attendance of skilled professionals during and after childbirth reduce the risk associated with these complications. Access to family planning services to prevent unwanted pregnancies is also essential (WHO 2007).

However, there are common obstacles to the effective delivery of these key elements in Africa. These obstacles act as bottlenecks to better provision and are particularly acute in rural settings or wherever else the state is largely absent. Three of these stand out:

Use of modern health services: Women or their families are often reluctant or unable to make use of available medical assistance, which creates obvious obstacles to timely diagnosis and treatment. The immediate factors at work include suspicion or ignorance of modern health services, prohibitive financial costs – due in part to distance – and weak incentives to use public health facilities.

Timeliness of emergency treatment: The lengthy time it takes to refer and transfer women to health facilities with the required technical capacity means emergency interventions come late. Obstacles include lack of accessible health infrastructure and failings in emergency evacuation procedures, such as ambulance services.

Shortcomings in the quality of care: Even when women reach appropriate health facilities, the quality of care available can hamper the treatment of complications. Quality is diminished by shortages of appropriately trained health staff, stock-outs of blood and medicines, absent equipment, poor staff motivation and low adherence to professional standards.

The obstacles that contribute to these bottlenecks must be overcome if maternal health outcomes are to improve. This entails technical solutions, but health-care providers, government and society must be open to these. Also required are innovations in policies and management arrangements, which are dependent in part on incentives and institutions that promote reform.

Similar conditions, uneven progress Malawi, Niger, Rwanda and Uganda differ in many respects but share conditions of general resource scarcity and all rely heavily on external resources to finance public health-care. They have followed similar approaches to health financing. All experimented with cost recovery in the 1990s and now favour some form of user-fee exemption. All have also implemented decentralisation measures to devolve finance and administration, including of the health service, to the local level. However, progress on national maternal health indicators over the past twenty years has been uneven.

Data on maternal mortality are subject to large uncertainties. and estimates differ between sources. According to the best inter-agency estimates, all of the countries in our study sample are in the group of twenty-four sub-Saharan African countries that achieved at least a 40% reduction in MMR over the two decades 1990 to 2010. This source gives estimated reductions of 47% (Uganda), 52% (Niger), 59% (Malawi) and 63% (Rwanda) (WHO et al. 2012). However, these numbers hide short-term variations (e.g. worsening rates in Malawi in the late 1990s), and do not capture within-country differences, such as the massive urban–rural differential in Niger (Vangeenderhuysen et al. 1995).

The Demographic and Health Surveys (DHS) use direct and indirect methods for gathering data on MMR over the seven years preceding each survey. The results are considered robust within stated margins of error, but have the disadvantage of sometimes irregular timing. According to this source (see Figure 3.1), MMRs for Malawi and Rwanda have fallen steeply since 2000. In Malawi, however, the gains barely recover the losses sustained during the 1990s. The changes between surveys for both Niger and Uganda are, in contrast, well within the margins of statistical error (UBOS and ICF International 2012).

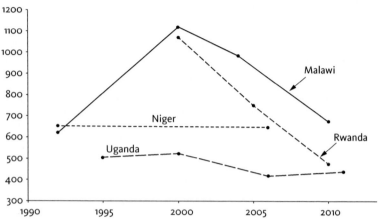

3.1 Maternal mortality ratios (deaths per 100,000 live births)

Source: ICF Macro and national statistical offices, Demographic and Health Survey final reports, various years

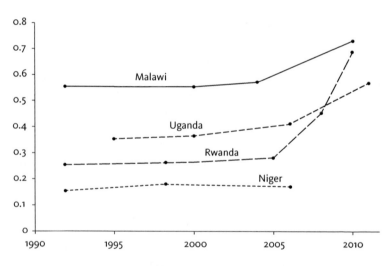

3.2 Deliveries at health facility

Source: ICF Macro and national statistical offices, Demographic and Health Survey final reports, various years

DHS data also give some indications on what is usually taken as the most important proximate cause of improvement in MMRs, namely the proportion of births that take place in formal health facilities (see Figure 3.2). On this measure, there have been significant recent improvements following negligible earlier changes in Malawi and Uganda. However, Rwanda has seen the most spectacular improvement, with an increase in the proportion of women giving birth in health facilities rising from 28% in 2005 to 69% in 2010 (NISR et al. 2012).

To the extent that these data on maternal health achievements suggest a pattern, with Rwanda emerging as the strongest performer, they pose important questions about causes. The APPP field studies (Cammack and Kanyongolo 2010; Olivier de Sardan et al. 2010a; Golooba-Mutebi 2011; Cammack 2012a; Chambers and Golooba-Mutebi 2012; Olivier de Sardan 2012b; Sabiti and Ssebunya 2012; Golooba-Mutebi forthcoming) amplify the picture. Based not on nationally representative sampling but on extended observation in purposively selected research sites, they document the extent to which the three main causes of maternal death identified above – use of modern health services, timeliness of emergency treatment, and shortcomings in quality of care – are being effectively addressed in different national and local settings. They then provide pointers to the institutional variations that appear to account for the most important differences, and finally to the broader aspects of the political context that appear to underlie these differences.

Use of modern services

The cross-country differences in knowledge of, and incentives to use, modern medical assistance appear substantial. In Rwanda, the fast-improving uptake of maternal health services appears to be a response to, among other things, very effective public education campaigns and powerful incentives. As we have seen, use of formal facilities seems to be increasing in Malawi and Uganda but the barriers to further improvement appear substantial, and with less reason in terms of physical distances and location of facilities than in Niger. Traditional birth attendants (TBAs) – the main alternative to formal midwifery – are now banned in all four countries, but they remain popular with local populations in Niger and Uganda, and are still practising in Malawi. Only in Rwanda, where TBAs were integrated into and subsequently replaced by the village community health system, have they effectively disappeared.

Pull and push factors in Malawi In Malawi, access to health facilities for giving birth is becoming easier as new clinics are built and more staff are employed, but there are powerful factors working against full realisation of the benefits. APPP fieldworkers identified five factors leading women not to attend health facilities to give birth: cultural practices, religious preferences, inadequate transportation, reluctance to go to overcrowded clinics run by unsupportive staff, and the continuing availability of TBAs near their homes.

Some Malawians avoid maternity services because they fear their foetuses will be 'stolen' through magical means by strangers at the clinics. Cultural beliefs play a role. Some believe that women who have extramarital sex while pregnant, or who have husbands who have multiple partners, will have their pregnancies 'tied' (closure of the birth canal) so that they will not be able to deliver normally. In such cases herbal medicine is required, but this is unavailable at modern facilities. In the research sites, there were also cases of women belonging to churches that offer alternative health-care and delivery methods, and which eschew modern medicine and clinics.

Women in labour living at a distance from clinics, or where roads in informal settlements are impassable, may never get an ambulance or make it to clinics. However, there are also factors discouraging contact with formal health services. In the research sites, there were widespread complaints of nurses, especially trainees, being 'rude' and 'arrogant'. Nurses were seen as giving preference to their friends and to richer women, and as demanding too much of the patients, often chastising women for not following health-service rules. 'A patient's dignity is stripped off and they become objects of abuse and laughter,' one new mother complained (Cammack and Kanyongolo 2010: 19).

In these and other cases, women turn to TBAs, who are said to be 'caring' and to 'show love to pregnant women, giving a lot of hope to women in pain during labour' (ibid.: 19n). Women also praise TBAs for being more patient with slow deliveries and for allowing women to deliver normally, rather than having to undergo Caesarean sections at hospitals. Though TBAs have been banned, they still practise because the ban is not enforced by the authorities. Former President Mutharika muddied the policy waters by declaring after a trip to the United Nations that the ban had been lifted. After that, it became even harder for the Ministry of Health to convince women who were reticent for various reasons to attend clinics to deliver.

Maternal death as 'fate' in Niger Not long ago the rate of maternal mortality in Niger was reportedly the highest in the world. Less risky maternity – essentially the possibility of doing a Caesarean section, of having blood supplies in case of emergencies and of handling ectopic pregnancies – has been available only recently and even today is accessible by only part of the population. In the past such services were not available at all in most rural areas, and childbirth was undertaken at home under conditions where the only recourse in case of complications was calling a *marabout* for prayers. Sometimes it still happens that way, partly for lack of facilities but also because many Nigériens still believe that only magico-religious practices can prevent deaths. If a death happens, it is an expression of fate (Olivier de Sardan et al. 2010a: 11–12).

Today the focus of the national policy on maternal health is to ensure the safe management of pregnancy and childbirth in public health facilities. High rates of death still occur for two general reasons. Either women deliver without the aid of professional service providers, staying at home out of preference or because in an emergency they cannot access the ambulance they need to reach the nearest formal health centre, often at considerable distance; or they attend health facilities with insufficient staff and equipment to tend to emergency cases. Major bottlenecks persist in all of these areas, as discussed below.

Weighing up the options in Uganda In Uganda maternal health services are provided by district health offices and by non-profit and private facilities run by faith-based organisations and NGOs, with subsidies from government. Health facilities range in size and complexity from small health centres in villages to clinics caring for 5,000–20,000 people, and to hospitals serving hundreds of thousands or even millions.

Popular attitudes about Caesarean sections and expectations about unsympathetic or overworked nurses mirror those found in Malawi. In theory, government health services are free, but in practice people must pay for transport, sometimes for drugs, probably for their food if inpatients, and sometimes fees to staff. Inability to make payment acts as a deterrent to accessing health services generally, not just for maternity care. In addition, transport to clinics is underdeveloped or non-existent (Golooba-Mutebi forthcoming). These factors serve as disincentives to attend facilities where modern care might be found.

In addition, women have alternatives to public services. These tend to be physically closer, cost less, have shorter waiting times and are better known. They include folk specialists, practitioners of traditional medicine, drug shops operated by variously trained people, and TBAs.

Women likely to need emergency interventions are supposed to be identified in the course of antenatal visits. However, in Uganda most women attend antenatal clinic once during their pregnancies to obtain a registration card, in case they need to use the health service later to deliver. Women are meant to bring their husbands when they first come to antenatal clinic, in order to be tested for HIV and to enrol any HIV-positive mother in a PMTCT (Prevention of Mother to Child Transmission) programme. However, most women come alone, saying that their husbands refuse to attend. Many women do not return for a second antenatal visit once they have their card. Whereas 94% of all pregnant women make one visit to antenatal clinics, only 42% make the recommended four visits. Those who do come have their first antenatal visit late in the pregnancy – at a median of 5.5 months – which is too late for some to benefit or to make follow-up antenatal visits (Uganda 2010: 23; Sabiti and Ssebunya 2012: 10, 20–1).

Government's attempts to induce women to attend clinics and hospitals to deliver babies have included banning TBAs, creating voluntary Village Health Teams (VHTs) to mobilise people to use government services, declaring maternity care to be free and establishing a health monitoring unit (MHSDMU) at central government level. These work against the disincentives listed above. However, APPP studies and other research indicate that the comprehensiveness of VHT mobilisation and sensitisation is variable. VHT members complain about lack of equipment and transport, about levels of supervision and feedback, and about working as volunteers without wages (Golooba-Mutebi et al. 2011).

Rwanda: education plus enforcement The way Rwanda tackles problems similar to those found in the three countries above illustrates our contention that exploring institutions in detail is required to understand how governance affects service delivery. The Rwandan government has created a set of hybrid institutions that incentivise health staff and ordinary citizens to abide by the policies as written. These policies differ little from those found in Malawi, Uganda and Niger – mostly because they reflect international standards and thinking – but the way they are implemented in Rwanda is very different (Chambers 2012; Chambers and Golooba-Mutebi 2012).

Inhabitants of all the villages studied were within an hour's walk of the nearest health centre and a three-hour walk of the nearest district hospital, which reflects the smaller size of Rwanda compared to, say, Niger, where long distances to facilities present a major health risk. With one exception, a Catholic health centre, no other non-state health-care alternative exists in any of the five 'sectors' (sub-districts) selected for study. This absence of alternative providers reduces the chances that women will go elsewhere for care, and will subject themselves to unregulated care as in Uganda and Malawi.

At the village level, district public health personnel are supported by volunteer Community Health Workers (CHWs) – not unlike VHTs in Uganda or health committees (mentioned farther on) in Malawi. Each village has four elected CHWs, one of whom is responsible for maternal health. Living in close proximity to their fellow villagers and undertaking household visits and participating in village meetings, CHWs raise household awareness of simple preventive health measures with the objective of promoting behavioural change. In the area of maternal health CHWs sensitise the population about the need to use family planning methods and for pregnant women to attend antenatal and post-natal consultations and to give birth at health centres. Villagers consider them authority figures and for the most part appear to accept and follow their instructions. Although CHWs have no mandate to impose sanctions on people, a popular perception is that they do.

Access to health-care services has been eased since Rwanda rolled out the community-based micro-insurance health scheme, the *mutuelle de santé*. Aware it could not offer good, free health-care to all, the Government of Rwanda created this non-profit venture providing health insurance for both formal and informal sector workers who fall outside other insurance plans. The payment of an annual fee, which varies according to income, entitles members to access free curative care after a one-off additional contribution by patients of just 200F (about 35 US cents in 2010) for an initial consultation. It also entitles them to free specialist care at district and national hospitals. The subscription enables women to access at an affordable cost a wide range of maternal health services, including deliveries, surgical interventions, pre- and post-partum hospitalisation, and ambulance services. The portion of the population subscribing to the scheme is high, ranging from 72% to 92% of the population in the APPP research areas (Chambers and Golooba-Mutebi 2012: 18).

Antenatal care is offered free of charge by all health facilities. During the first antenatal care visit, women are obliged to attend with their partners so they both undergo obligatory HIV and syphilis testing. In our field sites, this was generally complied with, in contrast with what was observed in Uganda. In all but two of the health facilities studied, HIV-positive expectant mothers were subsequently integrated into prevention of mother-to-child transmission programmes. A large number of pregnant women in both districts visited their health centres at least once to undertake antenatal visits. Across seven health centres antenatal coverage rates in 2009 varied between 60% and 100%, though the percentage of those making all four recommended antenatal visits remained low, as in Uganda (ibid.: 22).

The APPP Local Governance research confirmed what is generally understood internationally but so often ignored in recommending policies for Africa: that behavioural change in the field of public health is not induced simply by giving the population information about what is good for them. Changes such as raising the numbers of women giving birth under skilled care, increasing the uptake of family planning methods and getting people to subscribe to health insurance require an element of enforcement. In the two districts under study in Rwanda, a dual strategy has been adopted that marries public education campaigns with more forceful persuasion.

As almost everywhere in Africa, public education campaigns teach people the importance and benefits of adopting certain behaviours. Communities are 'sensitised' through government health education, focused collaborative campaigns and community mobilisation. But, importantly, sanctions are used to compel recalcitrant citizens to follow the recommendations, and rewards are given to acknowledge publicly the efforts of people who have adopted new patterns of behaviour. Sanctions take the form of fines imposed on those individuals or households that do not respect guidelines and exhortations, such as to give birth at clinics rather than at home, to attend antenatal sessions, or not to use traditional medicine and folk therapies.

In some areas fines have been regularised. In Musanze District, for example, in August 2010 a district council directive was published that detailed a list of punishable offences accompanied by their corresponding fines. It instructed local authorities to impose a fine of

2,000 francs (US$3.50) on women who give birth at home and who do not adhere to the requirement to undertake antenatal consultations. For non-payment of the mutuelle insurance fees, a 5,000-franc fine was introduced. On the other hand, incentives designed to induce behavioural change took the form of financial and in-kind gifts and were dispensed at the level of health facilities. In Nyamagabe District they included the payment of the first year of a child's health insurance, the exemption of pregnant women from paying delivery charges if they had undertaken four antenatal consultations, and occasional small gifts to women seeking post-natal care.

Non-financial sanctions are also used. In Musanze District the first week in December is known as 'mutuelle week'. During this time local authorities join forces with other local actors (including the police) to encourage people to subscribe to the national health insurance scheme. Pressure can be applied by blocking access to local markets to traders and customers who do not possess valid mutuelle cards. They also might check people in bars and other public areas to see if they can show evidence of having paid individual subscriptions.

In view of APPP's local observations, it is not at all surprising that the proportion of women giving birth in a clinical environment has increased steeply in Rwanda over the last five years. Only a few years ago, home births were considered to be the norm in the study villages. While it is not yet the case that all women deliver at health units, home deliveries are now more the exception than the rule. For example, in Nyamagabe District, local records suggest that the percentage of women birthing at Jenda health centre increased from 9% to 72% in the five-year period between 2004 and 2009 (ibid.: 19).

Among several other factors, government policy outlawing the activities of TBAs has contributed to this trend. Initially, government changed the role of TBAs from assisting women in labour to encouraging women to use health centres or accompanying those who were about to deliver to health facilities. However, this policy was eventually abandoned. Some of the younger, more literate, TBAs became CHWs. As for the rest, Rwanda has been exceptional in ensuring that no vestiges of TBA practice have remained.

Timeliness of emergency treatment

The feasibility of timely transfers to higher-level facilities for emergency interventions, such as Caesarean sections, appears to differ markedly across the countries. This bottleneck has remained severe in Niger and a significant challenge in Malawi and Uganda. In Rwanda, physical distances are typically less than in Malawi, Uganda and especially Niger. That said, transport challenges are not insignificant owing to Rwanda's hilly terrain. The Niger case is most illustrative of the issues that can prevent timely evacuation of emergency maternity cases.

Niger: ambulance provision and the 'extra pennies' initiative Given shortages of equipment and staff at rural clinics, the need for ambulance services to transfer emergency cases to better facilities is overwhelming in Niger. Emergency cases requiring urgent evacuation include eclampsia, pre-fracture syndrome, haemorrhages, obstructed labour, foetal distress, transverse presentation and placenta previa. Local health centres in Niger frequently do have ambulances at their disposal but patients have to pay for fuel and cover the expenses of drivers and security personnel, which often makes evacuation impossible, resulting in unnecessary deaths. This has not always been the case.

In 2003, with the agreement of the Health Management Committee representing users, the Directorate of Health for the region of Dosso took the initiative of collecting an 'additional penny', i.e. a sum of FCFA 100 (then about 17 US cents), from each patient attending a consultation at a health centre in the region. The purpose was to create a fund to support emergency transfers. This quickly proved effective. More than enough funds were raised, and they were placed in a special bank account. The practice of collecting 'extra pennies' then spread spontaneously to all the health districts of the country.

This arrangement, obliging all users of health centres to pay a modest tax for the purpose of assisting those needing evacuation, received a certain level of formal endorsement thanks to its approval by the district health teams and Health Management Committees. However, in 2009 the Ministry of Health took steps that threw the evacuation funds into crisis. It decided that this form of payment by users was contrary to official policy on user-charge exemptions, since users that were officially exempt were paying the extra penny like everyone else. It therefore banned health centres from collecting the 100 CFA francs for consultations involving children under five years old. Since the latter accounted for more than half the consultations, the funds collected fell significantly and the amount available for supporting ambulance services declined. Payment for evacuations reverted to the ambulance users and their families (Olivier de Sardan 2012b: 4–7; 2012a).

Private solutions in Uganda and Malawi In Uganda, there were no ambulances at the health centres studied by the APPP team. In an emergency, families were responsible for finding transportation to the next health unit for a woman in labour. While lack of resources may be to blame, there were indications in the study areas that the few ambulances available were routinely occupied in ferrying private goods. One had become the source of a conflict between a politician and health officials, which left it grounded at Kyamuliibwa police station (Sabiti and Ssebunya 2012: 25).

In peri-urban Ndirande in Malawi's commercial capital, Blantyre, the clinic was served by one ambulance. This was one of four that together were expected to cover the whole Blantyre district, including emergency deliveries to Queen Elizabeth Central Hospital in the city centre. At the time of the fieldwork, fuel shortages were acute, which reduced availability further. Making matters worse, the use of any vehicle was impossible in some of these neighbourhoods because the space between the roughly constructed houses was too narrow to pass, and the roads were too uneven and rocky. The ambulance was often unavailable when needed, so women had to find other ways to get to the clinic or hospital. That entailed walking or hiring a taxi, whose cost was prohibitive for the poorest residents. Women living in poverty in isolated corners of Blantyre's informal settlements were known to use local TBAs or female family members to help them deliver instead.

This situation was ripe for political exploitation, and in the run-up to the 2009 election one parliamentary candidate lent a minivan to the Ndirande clinic to serve as an ambulance. She promised to provide one full-time after the election. She won her seat and a vehicle was delivered within the year. This may have alleviated the situation somewhat, for some families.

Rwanda: a functioning system In Rwanda, emergency evacuation has been significantly assisted by the widespread adherence to the community health insurance scheme, the mutuelle. Whereas patients are expected to contribute towards the cost of evacuation by ambulance from clinics to district hospitals, the mutuelle health insurance covers 90% of the cost of evacuation for those with coverage. Voluntary Community Health Workers have also been issued with specially programmed mobile phones so they can contact health facilities for referral by sending text messages. Also, the increasing availability of 'waiting wards' for expectant mothers at rural health centres makes accidental home births less likely and enables the swift and early diagnosis of complicated deliveries. Thus, the risk of delays, due to lack of transport, in transferring emergency cases to hospital was rarely raised as a problem by either users or health staff.

Each of the three district hospitals in the APPP study had at least two ambulances and in Musanze District three of the four health centres had their own ambulances or shared with others. In all cases the running costs, maintenance and staffing of these vehicles were guaranteed by the relevant health facilities. Health centre records suggest that between 20% and 33% of expectant mothers are transferred to district hospitals, mostly in anticipation of specialist or surgical interventions. Transfers from home to clinics are less common, and they are provided for by hand-carried stretcher-ambulances (*ingobyi*) served by local volunteers, or by vehicles where the roads are better (Chambers and Golooba-Mutebi 2012: 21).

Quality of care

The contrast in service quality at local health facilities across the research sites in the four countries appeared quite stark. In Rwanda, basic quality issues seemed to be being addressed. Health centre opening hours were respected. Levels of hygiene appeared good. The research team reckoned that centre staff were generally respectful towards their patients. Monitoring and supervision visits were observed taking place. By contrast, even in the relatively favoured Ugandan central-south, health centres were subject to high levels of absenteeism, and opening hours were rarely respected. Fieldworkers in Uganda, Malawi and Niger found that staff attitudes towards patients were often demeaning and medical standards quite lax. Unable to absorb the increased numbers of women giving birth in health centres, facilities in Malawi and Uganda have suffered from severe overcrowding, overwhelming the capacity of frustrated and demoralised staff. In both countries, many public sector staff have been led to (and have been allowed to) open private facilities, some using government supplies, often while moonlighting from their public positions. This practice is banned in Rwanda.

Staff frustration and a failed remedy in Malawi The Malawi government is building new health facilities but there are still too few to serve the population. Similarly, while government is training more staff there are inadequate numbers of skilled nurses and midwives. As a result, overcrowding in some facilities is severe – with reports of unattended deliveries in maternity wards and women sleeping on the floor. Clinics are sometimes closed during opening hours, and stock-outs of drugs have been common in recent years. Staff are often overworked and demoralised and their frustration fuels their poor conduct towards women. In one incident at Ndirande clinic, a woman arrived at the clinic gate and delivered her baby in the dirt with the help of market women. Nurses inside the fence did nothing to help. This illustrates how bad the situation can become.

To induce women to leave their villages and present themselves at modern facilities to wait to deliver, the government is building maternity shelters at hospitals. Yet many of these are poorly constructed and maintained, and very unhygienic. Sharps and waste may be inadequately buried or incinerated near by.

Paralleling initiatives in other countries, the Malawi Ministry of Health has long supported voluntary health committees, which are meant to monitor staff and supplies at local health centres. However, they have not been a great success. The Ndirande clinic's Health Centre Committee is a case in point. There have been three such committees since the transition to multi-party rule in 1994, the first formed by political party representatives and the other two by people representing religious groups and chiefs. However, in each case committee members have complained of not receiving adequate training and of having confused lines of reporting and uncertain roles and powers.

Committee members became embroiled in conflicts with health workers over issues including late opening of the clinic; rude treatment of patients; poor management of drugs, food and mosquito nets; and suspected scams involving nurses' allowances. However, because of the lack of clarity over mandates, these disputes were unresolved, only generating ill-feeling. Since the committee members were unpaid, unsurprisingly their numbers dwindled and eventually the committees were disbanded. Some of the more general features of such experiences are discussed in Chapter 5.

Niger: technical deficiencies and absent staff In Niger, technical limitations on quality of care are often substantial. For instance, researchers found that Caesarean kits at various district hospitals were 'often incomplete and sometimes inappropriate' and anaesthetics were poorly supplied generally (Diarra 2009: 5–6). These deficiencies are partly caused and substantially deepened by staffing inadequacies. The result of insufficient staff is that many treatments are not carried out even when patients succeed in arriving at health centres for care, or the treatments are done by staff who are untrained in those specialisations. Our survey of clinics in the three small towns under study revealed critical gaps in medical staffing, some resulting from individuals abandoning their positions and others from personnel being transferred away without replacement.

Notoriously, some, especially female, carers who are assigned to rural clinics refuse to take up their posts because this would mean leaving their families behind in the city. In general, the farther the clinic from an urban centre, the bigger is the problem of staff shortages. Even where health officers take up their positions, some prefer to spend at least part of their time in urban centres and so are frequently absent (ibid.: 7–15).

Uganda: missing staff, missing equipment The situation in Uganda appears much like in Malawi and Niger, but with additional features that further undermine quality of care. Shortages of supplies, drugs and essential equipment are common. Almost all of the public health centres in the fieldwork areas were found to be lacking the basic equipment, such as weighing machines and 'delivery sets', which are needed to provide maternal health services effectively. In one health centre, there was one baby receiver, no suction machine, no catheter, and no stove for boiling its one pair of scissors. The nurse improvised by using ordinary bleach as a disinfectant. Some Health Centre IIIs (sub-county level) had no aprons for the midwives to wear, no gumboots, buckets, laboratories or reagents for testing for HIV. Clinics in remote areas had no electricity, which made vaccine storage dependent on solar- or gas-powered freezers. Without freezers, immunisation (e.g. for tetanus) was halted, as were maternal health services. Without fuel for lamps, clinicians told women in labour to buy paraffin or kerosene for light in order to deliver at night.

Cleanliness at the health units was found to be very poor. Compounds were unkempt and without incinerators. It was usual to see blood on floors and walls. Lack of water was common, especially during the dry season. In such circumstances, clinics have no water to bathe mothers who have just given birth. Even soap, disinfectant and detergents were often missing (Sabiti and Ssebunya 2012: 24–5).

The immediate factors behind poor services at facilities in Uganda include technical deficiencies (such as poor record-keeping and supervision, and insufficient or badly distributed funds). But they also include staff absenteeism and shortages, especially in rural postings, and the theft of major items of equipment as well as drugs and other highly portable supplies (Golooba-Mutebi forthcoming).

Rwanda: an impression of order and efficiency The situation in Rwanda is very different to that in the other three countries. On arrival at any of the numerous health facilities in Nyamagabe and Musanze Districts, the APPP researchers report, 'the first impression is ... of calm and order'. 'A series of low-level brick buildings with tiled or metal roofs are positioned around spotless courtyards, surrounded by immaculately kept landscaped gardens bordered with flowers and colourful trees. Clearly identifiable staff, dressed in white or blue overalls, move with purpose among the steady but manageable stream of patients' (Chambers and Golooba-Mutebi 2012: 11).

Thus, for instance, Cyanika health centre employs a full-time nurse responsible for undertaking prenatal consultations. The centre has a well-organised maternity wing with a waiting room reserved for women close to their due dates, a delivery room with an on-call nurse and a ward in which mothers and their newborn babies can recuperate. When the time comes the centre and its qualified nurses are fully equipped to deal with simple instances of childbirth and in the case of complications women can be transferred by the centre's ambulance to Kigeme hospital for specialist or surgical intervention.

In APPP's Rwandan research sites, not only is the infrastructure for health-care provision in place, but it is also well equipped and supplied to the necessary level. Human resource capacity appears to be of a professional quality, and through the Community Health

Workers system, the reach of the official health system extends right down to the community level. Geographical and financial access to health-care is improving; standards of general hygiene seem high; and the roll-out of integrated maternal health services seems well placed to continue. In short there is none of the poorly dispensed health-care, bad service and disorder that are to be found at many of the health facilities in Malawi, Uganda and Niger.

Institutional variations

How are we to explain these variations across research sites in four countries that share severe resource limitations and have been following similar policies? Making due allowance for geographical and environmental differences, why do the typical bottlenecks in improving maternal health appear to be being addressed quite effectively in Rwanda and less so in the other countries in our set? And what light does this shed on the central issue of this book: the type of governance that is most likely to work for development in Africa?

Reflecting on these questions in the course of fieldwork, we were led to the conclusion that most of the differences we observed could be explained by three variable features of the institutional arrangements governing maternal health-care:

- whether or not the de facto policy regime, including organisational mandates and resource flows, in the sector is internally coherent;
- the extent to which the national political leadership motivates and disciplines the multiple actors responsible for the quality of provision; and
- the degree to which there is an enabling environment that promotes or at least permits problem-solving at sub-national levels of the delivery system.

To anticipate the argument of later chapters, these factors were not only found to be sufficient for explaining differences in the health sector; they also were the critical variables affecting performance in the other three areas of public goods provision explored by the APPP Local Governance team (water and sanitation, markets and enterprise environment, and public order and security). The identification of these particular sources of institutional blockage led the whole research programme away from conventional thinking rooted in principal–agent theory and 'demand for good governance' and towards a more refined appreciation of what works to produce better public goods delivery in the context of Africa. For the moment, however, we remain focused on maternal health.

Policy coherence: Niger versus Rwanda

Across the four countries, policy processes are very uneven in terms of whether they deliver a coherent policy environment for efforts to improve maternal health. We limit ourselves here to the cases of Niger and Rwanda, which provide perhaps the strongest contrast.

Health policy in Niger has been for many years a particularly acute case of the general phenomenon of politically induced policy incoherence. In 2006, an overnight presidential decision to abolish user fees for pregnant women and under-fives nearly resulted in the collapse of the whole health system. The reform was implemented without the necessary accompanying measures. Increased demand for services and delayed payments by the state triggered severe cash-flow problems for primary health units. Because the measure was not well planned, and the financial resources to cover the costs associated with under-five care were not released by the state, after six years, the amounts owed by the state to health facilities had reached 1 billion FCFA. Every year this deficit grows larger. The delays affecting the reimbursements by the state threaten the whole health system. For example, many health facilities are heavily indebted to drug wholesalers, and many drugs are unavailable at clinics as a result (Olivier de Sardan et al. 2010b; Kafando et al. 2011).

A second example involves the experience with ambulance services to which we have already alluded. In 2004, to address the problem of emergency transfers of pregnant women and others, the Special Programme of the President of the Republic used HIPC funds to provide ambulances to all health districts in Niger. This programme was administered by the prefects completely outside the normal administrative channels and without any real coordination with the Ministry of Health. The Special Programme was a very politicised affair, disconnected from the country's regular planning procedures and serving essentially electoral purposes. It came to an end in 2010 when President Mamadou Tandja was removed from office by a military coup.

Between 2004 and 2010, the policy incoherence associated with this special arrangement generated a major bottleneck. While ambulances were now available, nothing had been arranged to cover their running costs, either by the President's Special Programme (which covered only the capital investment) or by the Ministry of Health (which had not been involved in the decision). Therefore, when there was a need for an emergency transfer the family of the patient had to find the money with which to pay the fuel costs and the per diem allowances of the driver, the health personnel accompanying the patient, and the Republican Guard soldier required for security. Raising the necessary funds could take time, and for many members of vulnerable families it was fatal.

The situation was especially paradoxical given that the state had adopted other measures to reduce financial barriers to obstetric referrals. Towards the end of 2005, President Tanja decided to make Caesarean sections free of charge, with the state reimbursing maternity referral centres for every Caesarean performed. But the transportation costs to referral centres, which remained the responsibility of users, typically exceeded the fee for the operation (35,000 FCFA – then about US$70), and could easily run as high as 50,000 CFA francs. In more inaccessible areas, the costs could be significantly higher (for example, between 150,000 and 200,000 CFA in Ngourti) (Diarra 2009: 15–21; Olivier de Sardan 2012a).

Farther on, we return to the interesting experience in sub-national problem-solving that tried to address this inconsistency in the national policy. A relevant observation here is that when the Ministry of Health put an end to the initiative, it did so in the name of policy coherence. Even though this brought the ambulance service to a standstill, the exemptions for under-fives had to be maintained! However, the coherence maintained was purely formal and had little relationship to the real situation on the ground for poor families. This illustrates the point that what matters for improving performance is de facto or on-the-ground policy coherence, not purity of policy doctrine.

Rwandan policy in the health sector provides a reassuring contrast. On the whole, policy reforms in Rwanda have been mutually reinforcing. Key aspects include: a reform of boundaries and mandates covering the whole country and all line ministries; a health-care reform in which incentives appear consistent (affordable health insurance plus strong pressure to use it); and a donor coordination arrangement that seems to be working down to district level (Chambers and Golooba-Mutebi 2012: 25–9).

In 2005, decentralisation and administrative reforms established new jurisdictions that in health at least seem functional and coherent. For instance, the location of health centres was a major factor in delimiting the territorial boundaries of administrative divisions, which means that lines of administrative and technical responsibility for health services facilities are unusually clear. Significant sectoral policy reforms and strategies were developed in coordination with the decentralisation policy to improve local service delivery in the health sector. Local governments have technical departments responsible for implementing local- and national-level policies. Employees of the technical departments are civil servants selected through a competitive recruitment process. At each local government level they report to their respective councils with the supreme authority being the district council. As we have seen, the use of voluntary Community Health Workers alongside strong encouragement to subscribe to the nationwide health insurance scheme, the mutuelle, has been critical to local uptake of maternal health services.

In 2006 the Rwandan government sought to bring further coherence to decentralised institutions by designing an aid policy that requires that all development assistance is monitored by the Ministry of Economic Planning and Finance (MINECOFIN) to ensure its delivery is harmonised with national and sector policies and that it promotes equitable sectoral and regional development (MINECOFIN 2006). Government-led sector-wide planning has also ensured that donor support plugs real resource gaps. The upshot is that each sector has a limited number of donor agencies to manage. In 2010 donors were also prohibited from working in more than three sectors. Control reaches to the district level, where the Common Development Fund (CDF) ensures that development assistance is aligned with the district development plans and that donors coordinate and report on their activities through participation in each district's Joint Action Development Forum.

In summary, the Rwandan government's commitment to improving maternal health has been reflected in consistent national- and local-level objectives and programmes, single-mindedness in pushing through policy reforms, and an effort to align policy reforms, funding arrangements and implementation strategies. It provides a striking example of how sustaining reforms that many African countries find extremely challenging is not impossible if the circumstances are right.

Politically enforced performance disciplines

Something similar applies to the second difference we have been led to emphasise. The level of enforcement of performance disciplines within public service, and related issues to do with the regulation of private provision, explain much of the observed differences in intermediate outcomes across the APPP study countries. The main differences relate directly to the presence or absence of strong upward accountability mechanisms, *not* to the presence or absence of downward accountability to health service users. The cases of Niger, Uganda and Rwanda best illustrate the relevant differences.

As we have seen, major bottlenecks in provision for maternal health in Niger are produced by staffing gaps, and not all of these are caused by national shortages of qualified staff. They have to do with deficiencies in human resource management, which are at root political. Throughout the sector, coherent management of staff postings is extremely difficult, with the result that rural health units are often understaffed and urban ones overstaffed. Efforts by managers to correct these anomalies are routinely undermined when midwives and medical personnel 'pull strings' in the capital to get them overturned. In one site, the level of incompetence and indiscipline among staff who play a key role in the treatment of maternity cases is extreme. This is well understood and there are regular complaints about it by more senior staff and users of the facility.

In one particular facility, an especially undisciplined and ill-trained senior midwife is one of a group of 'untouchables' maintained in post by the patronage of the local canton chief with the connivance of the sector hierarchy (Diarra 2009: 7–15; Olivier de Sardan et al. 2010a: 20, 25). This was just one instance – a particularly dangerous one for the pregnant women exposed to it – within a human resource management system that was, and no doubt remains, shot through with political string-pulling and preferential allocation of postings.

In Uganda, evidence from case studies in Masaka and Rakai Districts and spot checks in other parts of the country indicate high levels of both understaffing and absenteeism in state health facilities (Golooba-Mutebi forthcoming). Many staff are typically absent. Facilities that are supposed to be open twenty-four hours may be accessible for five hours per day, leaving people to wait for some time before staff arrive. In Uganda, this state of affairs is at least in part the result of staff being allowed to run their own clinics and health shops (Golooba-Mutebi et al. 2011: 37; Golooba-Mutebi forthcoming: 5).

While public sector staff were found to complain of poor remuneration, comparisons with private not-for-profit (e.g. church-run) facilities suggests the problem has different roots. In fact, church-affiliated facilities (which are often preferred by patients) find it hard to retain staff because the equivalent government health units pay better, have shorter effective working hours, and allow staff to have second jobs (Golooba-Mutebi et al. 2011: 31; Sabiti and Ssebunya 2012: 27–8). The incentive for disgruntled service users to apply pressure to improve state performance is likely weakened by the availability of private facilities, including those run by the same government staff.

The supervision that might be expected to control these abuses is largely absent (Golooba-Mutebi et al. 2011: 31; Golooba-Mutebi forthcoming). Similarly, misappropriation of medicines and informal charging for 'free' services are commonplace because there is in practice no active technical oversight and no system of professional performance incentives. Senior personnel do not perform their supervisory functions and justify this by citing logistical challenges and lack of vehicles. The health unit management committees that are supposed to watch over providers in their areas are defunct in many places. And, as noted previously, the voluntary community-based health committees have largely collapsed, and so offer none of the management support that they were designed to provide.

While many of Rwanda's policies are similar to those found elsewhere, what sets the country apart is that there they are implemented with some rigour (Chambers and Golooba-Mutebi 2012: 29–37). First of all, active steps are taken to ensure that regulations and professional standards are respected and that national policies are implemented. In Nyamagabe and Musanze Districts, formal monitoring and supervisory mechanisms were seen to be in place at different levels and between entities answering to local authorities. Doctors from Kaduha and Musanze district hospitals, for instance, conduct monthly clinical supervision visits and pay weekly visits to administer anti-retroviral treatments to patients at each of the health centres within their jurisdictions. All the hospitals and health centres have Ministry of Health community health supervisors and coordinators, and the latter pay regular visits to Community Health Workers and participate in training sessions at local levels. Supervisors actively encourage their juniors to implement policies, for instance, requesting staff to update them on rates of mutuelle registration and demanding explanations for low rates.

Supervision plays an essential role in improving performance. In Musange sector, Nyamagabe District, during 2010 the health committee identified Community Health Workers' laxity and lack of authority as a key factor in the persistently high number of women giving birth at home. Health committee members adopted a two-pronged approach to addressing the problem. On the one hand, community health workers were criticised for their slackness and poor results during a CHW cooperative meeting. On the other hand, the health committee outlined for CHWs the support that the local authorities could provide them with whenever community members refused to adopt the practices government was advocating.

A second factor maintaining performance disciplines is a set of consistent incentives. As regards health sector employees, three features seem particularly crucial. First of all, salaries are normally paid on time. Secondly, health professionals employed by the state are not allowed to run private health-care facilities, and so do not have the option of moonlighting. Thirdly, all public health facilities are subject to quarterly assessments which are the basis for performance-based rewards and sanctions.

Performance bonuses can represent a significant 20% difference in a hospital doctor's monthly salary. Alternatively these awards are used collectively to encourage staff to find innovative ways of implementing health policies. One health centre invested its bonuses in the purchase of presents to distribute to women who gave birth at the health centre because a clinic receives a financial award for every child born in their facility and this strategy helped increase their overall award. Staff in another health centre, understanding that every child born at home would represent a reduction in their award, introduced a 'commission' of 500F to be paid to a Community Health Worker every time the CHW accompanied a pregnant woman to the health centre to give birth.

Even volunteer Community Health Workers are incentivised, which counteracts the tendency found elsewhere that sees villagers quit such jobs. First, CHWs have been encouraged to form income-generating cooperatives in which the performance-based financing paid to them is invested. When visited by APPP researchers, some of these cooperatives were well advanced in starting income-generating projects. Secondly, some Community Health Workers were receiving indirect financial benefits, such as the payment of their family *mutuelle de santé* subscriptions, or were gaining access to interest-free loans to pay for them. Other incentives include financial rewards for accompanying pregnant women to a health centre to give birth; free access to equipment that they need to do their work (such as telephones, umbrellas and plastic boots); and prizes, such as radios given by the health centre to reward good work.

Unlike health-service staff, local authority personnel do not receive any financial incentives besides their salaries. However, the introduction of the *imihigo*[1] (performance contracts) has added an element of evaluation to their work. Imihigo provides a system of moral rewards and sanctions drawing on neo-traditional principles. It is applied to the public service at all levels, nationwide. In this case, under imihigo local officials pledge publicly to achieve certain objectives, including public health targets.

The use of imihigo to drive up performance levels has also encouraged a sense of competitiveness among local authorities that strive for the prestige and status attached to the receipt of certificates of merit and the winning of trophies awarded to good performers. Some district councils where performance has consistently fallen below standard have sacked the responsible senior officials. For local officials, career progression and the ability to keep a job are increasingly dependent on their own and their districts' good performance.

In Rwanda, then, upward accountability mechanisms have been accompanied by consistent incentives – moral and material rewards and sanctions – that ensure that actors, both citizens and staff, are

---

1 The concept of *imihigo* dates back to the sixteenth century and refers to the traditional practice of warriors making public pledges to their kings to engage in specific accomplishments, to test their bravery. Imihigo was undertaken in a competitive spirit, with pride and enhanced status as the rewards of success, while failure was not punished. The concept was revived in 2005 as an accountability mechanism to provide incentives to local government leaders and their populations to meet local and national development targets. An annual imihigo contract is signed between the President of the Republic and the district mayors based on national and local priorities and specific objectives, selected by the district, backed by measurable performance indicator targets. Performance is evaluated on an annual basis and the mayor must report back publicly to the president on the progress towards the objectives.

motivated and work towards the same goals. The drivers behind these arrangements are, as we explain later, political.

Scope for local problem-solving

Locally coordinated actions to address delivery bottlenecks are present in some contexts in all four countries. However, there are differences in the scope of feasible local initiatives, how institutionalised local problem-solving is and how well any achievements at local level are integrated with national policy processes. Niger and Rwanda represent two contrasting patterns, at least with respect to the case of maternal health. We provide a broader treatment of issues of local problem-solving and grassroots collective action in Chapter 5.

The 'extra pennies' initiative in Niger, to which we have alluded twice already in this chapter, is an example both of local problem-solving and of the state undermining local initiative. It was not informal but institutionalised to the extent that it was validated by the district health management teams and Health Management Committees. It was an institutionalised response from below to the incoherence of the public health policy on emergency transfers. But it was quite different from the type of solutions that result from a deliberate policy or joint initiative of the state and international agencies. The scheme was fully developed 'from below', without consultation with the ministry, or any agreement or support from that quarter. That was its strength, but given the small space allowed for local problem-solving within the policy system presided over by the Government of Niger and Niger's international donors, it was also its weakness. The scheme was scrapped in spite of its revealed benefits (Olivier de Sardan 2012b: 6–7).

On the other hand, Rwanda, in spite of its reputation for authoritarianism, provided the APPP researchers with the best example of the institutionalisation of local problem-solving. Local coordination and citizen participation have been important features of the Rwandan change model, not just in principle, as elsewhere, but also in practice. A network of advisory and oversight committees provides a space for collaboration and coordination between the different local-level actors. These committees not only help to ensure that everyone is working towards the same objectives. They also allow bottlenecks to the achievement of overall goals to be discussed and acted upon (Chambers and Golooba-Mutebi 2012: 37–49).

Within health facilities, management committees, management boards and health committees supervise work. Health centres' health committees consider matters brought to their attention by management committees and approve decisions made by them. These higher management units include representatives from the health facility, the local authority and civil society (or, in church-affiliated units, the clergy). A hospital management committee consists of the hospital's senior managers and departmental heads, while a hospital management board includes the hospital director and district executive secretary, and representatives from the private sector, civil society and the district. While not unusual in form, these arrangements do seem unusually vibrant and to produce a high degree of communication and coordination across the sector.

On a more modest scale, some of the institutional initiatives that the Rwandan state has been using to promote development efforts at community level have an element of institutionalised local problem-solving. Like imihigo, *ubudehe mu kurwanya ubukene* (collective action to combat poverty) and *umuganda* (communal work) are neo-traditional concepts which have been blended with modern techniques for participatory problem identification and action.

Ubudehe has been used as part of a national poverty eradication initiative. Implementation starts with classification of poor people, thereby enabling the poorest and most vulnerable households to be identified by their fellow villagers. In this way, they become the priority recipients of any support available from the government or its development partners, including payment of mutuelle subscriptions, thereby extending health insurance coverage – and, along with it, free deliveries – to the poorest households.

Umuganda is a monthly exercise in self-help designed to address an issue or need of common interest to the residents of specific localities. On the last Saturday of the month people come together to clean public spaces or build or repair infrastructure. The idea is not new, but was used extensively by the pre-genocide Habyarimana regime before dying away as multipartyism became the dominant political idea (Uvin 1998). It involves, of course, a form of non-progressive taxation, but in the context may serve several useful social functions.

As noted earlier, such activities provide occasions on which local authorities and health professionals can educate the public about a wide range of issues, including those related to maternal health. There is also a problem-solving element. It is no accident that Rwandan health facilities and villages give an impression of cleanliness and order. The physical deterioration of buildings and equipment and the accumulation of garbage, which in the other study countries are among the many issues that these days (although not in the past) are systematically neglected, are addressed in Rwanda as umuganda projects. Though this may surprise some readers – as it did a number of APPP researchers – Rwanda today may exemplify the kind of balance between corporate bureaucratic discipline and local participatory processes that is lacking in our other present-day country studies (Chambers and Golooba-Mutebi 2012: 49–52).

Why Rwanda?

Our suggestion is, then, that Rwanda is making better progress than Malawi, Niger or Uganda at addressing the major barriers to improving maternal health, and this at two levels. First, in Rwanda there is more evidence of a real effort to deal with the three internationally recognised bottlenecks to better provision: insufficient use of modern services, lack of timely access to emergency treatment and poor quality of care in health facilities. Secondly, Rwanda is doing better in three areas which we have identified as critical to the institutional context: policy coherence, politically enforced performance disciplines and support to local problem-solving. Thus, it is no accident that while the DHS estimates of MMRs and births in health facilities show that things are improving in most countries of our set, the scale of the recent improvements in Rwanda is unmatched.

The finding that Rwanda is getting better results and achieving them because of a more favourable set of institutional arrangements was surprising to many in the APPP team. Much of the research-based literature on Rwanda gives a picture of the country's local governance under the RPF-led regime that is highly unattractive and suggestive of anything but inclusive and effective social provision. But the solution to the paradox lies not so much in any mistaken appreciation of the nature of the regime in Kigali, but in the assumptions that social researchers typically bring with them about the kind of institutions that are most likely to work for development in Africa. Typically, international researchers judge Rwandan arrangements by the standards that they have learned about in their home countries. Local researchers tend to follow their lead. The whole issue testifies to the inability of the ahistorical 'good governance' agenda to specify correctly what matters in governance for development.

A crucial step in our argument has been to infer from the differences in treatment of immediate bottlenecks across research sites and countries that three, and only three, intermediate variables matter – policy coherence, provider disciplines and local problem-solving. We have not emphasised the weakness of 'demand-side' pressures on service providers, because we did not find them to be evident to any great extent or remotely as important as top-down disciplines. We have not focused on decentralisation, because all our country cases have decentralisation policies and we found that what makes the difference is the level of politically driven coherence and discipline that is put into the running of local services. The well-documented fact that Rwanda is not a hospitable environment for free-wheeling NGOs and critical journalism has concerned us less than it concerns many observers because in the field we did not see any connections between solving the problems we have observed on the ground and the magic bullet of 'social accountability'.

It may be less obvious that our interpretation has been free of elements of the older, so-called 'supply side', variant of conventional principal–agent thinking. As we have seen, an important element in the way health providers are motivated in the current Rwandan system is performance-based financing of health units. Performance-based financing, along with performance contracts for senior civil servants (an aspect of imihigo), are favoured remedies at the World Bank and pure products of traditional top-down principal–agent strategies to improve bureaucratic performance. However, our finding is not that these things work in Rwanda and therefore ought to work everywhere. On the contrary, they work in Rwanda because of specific contextual and design features.

First, they are part of a package that includes both moral and material incentives and sanctions. The government has comprehensively and quite deliberately addressed social dilemmas such as free-riding, information gaps, conflicting and ineffective norms and rules, and disempowerment. It has drawn on half-remembered traditions together with imported 'best practice' methods to construct hybrid institutions that seem to work in promoting performance. Secondly, the whole package has very powerful political backing of a kind that is generally absent in the other study countries, at least in the present period. It benefits from aid funding but the donors have been subordinated to the country system to an extent that has not happened elsewhere in our set of countries.

Both aspects have to do with the nature of the regime in Kigali. Here, what matters is not what is usually emphasised in discussions of types of regime in Africa, but something else. The something else centres on the extent to which the Rwandan regime is the result of the solution of elite-level collective action problems that have not been solved in other countries, at least not recently. It has to do with the nature of the 'political settlement' or fundamental elite bargain that has come to prevail in the years since the 1994 genocide and more particularly since 2000, when Paul Kagame became president, and 2003, when a new power-sharing constitution was inaugurated. The normal donor complaints about a government's lack of vision or 'political will' to reform maternal health are not heard in Rwanda.

As we discuss at more length in Chapter 4, conventional regime classifications such as the distinction between 'dictatorships' and 'democracies' do not capture the factors that are most relevant to explaining differences in development performance in Africa. This is partly because, beneath a democratic veneer, most multiparty political systems remain substantially authoritarian as well as neopatrimonial in the sense that politics is largely about clientelism and private rent capture, not the provision of public goods. Used as a blanket characterisation, neopatrimonialism explains little. But APPP studies have found that there are more and less developmental forms of neopatrimonialism. We argue that there is a more developmental subtype of neopatrimonial regime, which is characterised by centralised management of the main economic 'rents' in support of a long-term vision. We have called this 'developmental patrimonialism' (Kelsall 2013).

Under such regimes, the ruling elite has the disposition and capacity to use rents productively to enlarge the national economic pie, rather than simply take the largest slices from it in the short term. Where this happens, policies and their implementation are aligned with the national vision, and key elements of the state technocracy are subjected to corporate disciplines. Anti-corruption efforts become more than a charade. These things happen, however, only when members of the national elite are motivated by some existential shock or threat to take steps to overcome the collective action problems that ordinarily keep them focused on factional or private interests within a very short time-horizon. Current regimes in Africa where this has happened include, and may be restricted to, Ethiopia and Rwanda.

In the Rwandan case, rent centralisation includes using the rents available to party-owned and army-owned companies to cover the learning costs involved in reviving and upgrading the private sector of the economy. Members of the political class are subject to collective disciplines that are enforced thanks in part to the ability of the ruling party to finance politicians' campaigns from company profits (Booth and Golooba-Mutebi 2012). This enables the state bureaucracy and public services to be protected from clientelistic capture by individual members of the political elite.

Thanks to these elements of the prevailing elite bargain or political settlement, the relationship between the government leadership and the civil service, including front-line health service providers, begins to approximate to the model assumed by principal–agent theory. But this happens only because the more fundamental problem of elite collective action has been solved, and this in turn has permitted a relatively high level of coordination of efforts vertically and horizontally throughout the government system. Rwanda is therefore the exception that confirms the rule that development problems are fundamentally about solving collective action problems and only secondarily and conditionally about principal–agent and information asymmetry issues.

Summing up

This chapter has used the delivery of safe motherhood to illustrate the manner in which governance institutions affect the behaviour of actors and, ultimately, development outcomes. In the Niger, Malawi and Uganda cases, improvements in maternal mortality rates have been registered, but not as quickly as in Rwanda. While the four countries' policies are similar, the way they are implemented differs widely.

Three factors go some way towards explaining why this is the case. In Rwanda, there have been deliberate attempts at the centre to bring coherence to the various policies that affect maternal care, including bringing donors and NGOs into line. In the other countries, there is a good deal of policy-induced institutional incoherence. In Rwanda, political competition is not allowed to undermine the formal national vision, and the national vision is forcefully transmitted to all parts of the implementation system. Traditional and modern forms of top-down performance monitoring, incentives and sanctions are blended in ways that motivate government staff to do their jobs properly and ordinary people to change their behaviour in beneficial ways. This is not the case in any of the other three countries currently. Finally and more unexpectedly, leaving scope for local problem-solving appears to be institutionalised in several ways in the Rwandan governance set-up, whereas we have found it to be either absent or fragile in the face of a perverse official concept of policy coherence in the Niger context.

This comparative analysis of public goods provision for maternal health has introduced two elements for further discussion. The first is the three-part hypothesis about important institutional blockages to provision – policy coherence, provider discipline and local problem-solving. In the following chapters, we show how this framework captures the key variables affecting public goods bottlenecks across a wider range of public goods and countries. The other is the discussion of ultimate political determinants that we have begun in answering the question 'why Rwanda?' In the following chapters, we deepen this discussion with reference to study countries whose politics are, for better or worse, unlikely to resemble those of Rwanda in the foreseeable future. Chapter 4 does this by undertaking a more wide-ranging discussion of problems of policy incoherence and provider discipline in public goods provision. Chapter 5 focuses on local problem-solving, the role of hybrid institutional solutions and the enabling environment for both.

4 | THE POLITICS OF POLICY INCOHERENCE AND PROVIDER INDISCIPLINE

In Chapter 3, we looked in detail at the factors influencing public provision of maternal health-care in Malawi, Niger, Rwanda and Uganda, drawing some conclusions about the institutional and political determinants of the main differences in performance. These conclusions have begun to show how it makes sense to see development challenges in terms of unresolved problems of collective action, rather than as a matter of some people democratically 'demanding' and other people more or less reluctantly 'supplying' public goods and services.

A great deal of what we have concluded about maternal health also applies to the other areas of public provision with which the APPP Local Governance research was concerned: water and sanitation, market regulation and public security. In this chapter we show how. This leads us to consider more explicitly why African democracies fail to provide a 'demand-side' solution to these problems on account of multilevel problems of collective action.

We begin the chapter by examining more broadly problems of policy incoherence and weak coordination among organisations charged with delivering public policies. This discussion refers particularly to examples from Malawi and Niger. We conclude with a suggestion about the first-level causes of typical forms of policy incoherence, emphasising the perverse interactions between populist policy-making styles and changing international policy fashions.

The chapter then looks more closely at provider indiscipline, drawing on APPP-documented experiences in Senegal, Sierra Leone and Tanzania, as well as examples from Malawi, Niger and Uganda. Although notorious today in most of the countries in our set, weaknesses of professional discipline among public service providers have in fact shown considerable variation over time. To some extent they also vary across sectors. However, we argue that the differences do not correspond to comfortable and conventional assumptions about political causes. Democratic openings under current African conditions tend to loosen disciplines, not to tighten them. There are good theoretical reasons for this, which we set out before telling the specific story of how Malawi's transition from a single-party to a multiparty political system has impacted on the delivery of public goods in the fields of water supply and markets.

The politics of policy incoherence

Under today's conditions of economic and political liberalisation, almost all public goods provision in Africa takes the form of *co-production* by several actors, including both formal organisations and informal collaborations between individuals or groups (Joshi and Moore 2004; Olivier de Sardan 2009b; Titeca and de Herdt 2011). Typical delivery configurations cut across the public and private sectors and involve some measure of formal or informal privatisation of what was once public provision (Blundo 2006; Blundo et al. 2006; Blundo and Le Meur 2008; Olivier de Sardan 2008a; Workman 2011a). As a result, even official state providers are subject to multiple pressures and accountabilities, not just the bureaucratic type emanating from the state (Blundo 2012).

An important issue affecting the quality of the provision is whether the co-production in question is based on a real coordination of efforts among the actors, and on incentives that are consistent. As we saw in relation to maternal health, a common pattern is one in which organisations and the individuals who work in them face unmanageable pressures because official policies and initiatives (e.g. on user charges) have passed in and then out of favour without ever being fully implemented, properly wound up or comprehensively replaced. A closely related problem is where the past history of public sector reforms has left a situation where organisational mandates and jurisdictions are so ill defined that they make even minimal levels of coordination among different agencies extraordinarily difficult.

In several fields of public goods provision, APPP researchers found that efforts to address key bottlenecks were being obstructed by one or both of two types of policy-driven institutional incoherence: confused mandates or overlapping jurisdictions among some or all of the organisations concerned; and perverse incentives confronting actors within particular organisations as a result of the incomplete implementation of a policy or the simultaneous pursuit of several policies that are, for practical purposes, in conflict. Malawi provides a particularly striking example of the first kind of incoherence, and Niger of the second.

City administration in Blantyre, Malawi In Malawi, the researchers were generally struck by the extent to which the boundaries of urban planning areas, agricultural development divisions, health departments and educational zones do not coincide. The jurisdictions and mandates of parastatals, elected politicians, chiefs and city authorities overlap in ways that produce confused responsibilities. This fragmentation of authority makes action in pursuit of a common goal hard to achieve.

A particularly acute example is the situation in Ndirande, Malawi's oldest peri-urban informal settlement. The Ndirande neighbourhood is one of the largest, poorest, least developed and most chaotic areas of Blantyre, the commercial centre of the country.

The suburb sits within the (Blantyre-Limbe) city boundary, so it is within the city's planning area. This means the city is responsible for its regulatory framework, physical upkeep and facilities management. At the same time, Ndirande is a conglomeration of old villages that were formally absorbed as the city population grew and the city's boundary was extended. Only a part of it (Newlines and Goliyo) was ever pegged off by land surveyors and turned into formal housing areas. So much of Ndirande remains as it always was: with unsurveyed and untaxed plots, unplanned and untended roads and pathways, urgently constructed water supply systems, no liquid sanitation pipes and few public facilities. Once public areas have been encroached upon by neighbours, sold off by chiefs or grabbed by powerful people (Njamwea 2003). The end result is an overcrowded, down-at-heel, higgledy-piggledy landscape overseen by local headmen and chiefs who retain ill-defined powers.

There are seven village headmen in Ndirande and the township is divided between them. The suburb is split between two MPs with different party affiliations. It falls within the city boundary but city officials show little interest in the area because relatively few residents pay property taxes (rates). Sector ministries, multiple parastatals and city authorities have responsibilities in the area but it is just one of many slums in Blantyre, all of which are crying out for help. Finally, any single arena – such as health, water or sanitation – has many actors whose mandates overlap. Add to that long-term resource shortages and it is easy to see why, administratively, Ndirande falls between the cracks.

The near-absence in Ndirande of city or state officials on a daily basis supports the notion that chiefs are in control. Many of the tasks normally done by civil servants – such as overseeing neighbourhood watch committees, holding court or signing formal documents for banks and passport offices – are done by chiefs and recognised by other authorities. That said, a chief's control is limited in practice by MPs and other local politicians as well as District Commissioners (DCs). But their relationships vary by time and place, and there are no hard and fast rules about what a chief may be permitted or required to do.[1] Party politics also plays a role – a chief close to a president, for instance, may be allowed great leeway, while one who is seen as having crossed the party in power may well find his powers curtailed.

In Ndirande, it is close to impossible to address water and sanitation challenges because of a complex web of coordination and resource problems. Because the city government has little capacity, the central state in the form of environmental officers attached to the Ministry of Health's district health office (DHO) plays a role in the settlement. It was they, for example, who organised a latrine survey in late December 2010 after a failed attempt by the city earlier in the year. But the DHO's environmental office itself is subject to constraints. For instance, it claimed not to have the resources to travel the few kilometres to Ndirande and check on toilet closures a few weeks after its survey was done.

Collaboration among those responsible for community outreach and identifying hazards in state and city offices is poor. Reportedly, relations between the Health Surveillance Assistants (HSAs)[2] from the DHO and those from the city have deteriorated as their terms and conditions and training backgrounds have diverged. Each set of HSAs reports to a different office and this has encouraged a habit of not sharing reports and otherwise undermined teamwork (Cammack 2012a: 18). One of the particular issues affected by this state of affairs is the condition of the Nasolo river.

The Nasolo: 'a river that no one owns' One of Blantyre's industrial zones sits astride the Nasolo river, which is known for its heavy-metal

---

1 For instance, they will identify needy claimants for aid, help distribute fertiliser subsidies, meet with civil servants and NGOs about development issues, be asked to meetings to represent their communities, and oversee electioneering during campaigns.

2 HSAs are health and environmental outreach officers working in the community. They give training on, and monitor, health and sanitation issues, distribute chlorine to purify water and organise health campaigns (e.g. maternal and childcare, vaccinations, etc.).

pollution (lead, cadmium, iron, phosphate, zinc, chromium, nickel, etc.). A short distance upstream is Ndirande, which houses many industrial and service workers, a few original settlers (*nzika*) and many newly arrived rural migrants seeking work and cheap accommodation.

Ndirande's residents claim that as late as the 1980s they were able to draw water for household use from the river, but that after the democratic transition in 1994 – with its relaxation of rules, including urban planning regulations – overcrowding and pollution put an end to that. Today residents next to the river release effluent from their bathhouses and latrines, while residents without latrines in their compounds throw plastic bags with faeces – 'flying toilets' – into the river and elsewhere (*Daily Times*, 21 March 2012).

Nonetheless, children play in the water and women still use the river to wash clothes; some collect water for their households from springs that bubble up along its banks. As late as 2009, restaurateurs were being warned by the market master to stop washing foodstuffs, cutlery and plates in the river. Cleaners use river water to wash the market, and dump market waste over its banks owing to a shortage of city skips.

At intervals between 2009 and 2011, APPP researchers questioned environmental officers at Blantyre city offices and at the Ministry of Health's DHO about river pollution in the city. The usual response was that city workers had planned to clean the Nasolo but had not done so as manpower was needed elsewhere. As mentioned above, the DHO surveyed the toilets that drain into the river in late 2010, but they did not return to check whether their owners had complied with warnings to stop discharging waste into the river. Chiefs whose villages adjoin the river said they had never thought of cleaning it. The market master in charge of Ndirande's main market claimed to be unaware that his staff were throwing garbage into it. When asked who cleans the river, women using it to wash clothes responded 'the rain is our City. The rains clear the rubbish and wash it down the river' (Cammack and Kanyongolo 2010: 42). Only a few residents have made any effort to deal with the pollution. One living next to the Nasolo placed a sign threatening to fine anyone throwing litter over its banks. In that spot it is relatively clean, but elsewhere the river and banks are filthy. Not surprisingly, there are outbreaks of cholera in most years and diarrhoeal diseases are common.

Ndirande residents tend to think that managing the river is the city's business. In fact, city environmental health officers accept it as their responsibility, but the city's capacity to do any work in Ndirande is reduced by its ongoing staff shortages and other resource constraints. Also, as mentioned previously, it prefers to work in areas where rates (land taxes) are paid and taxpayers demand services, rather than in squatter settlements. Staffing throughout local government has been affected by an informal freeze on hiring for some years. The politicisation of DC and Chief Executive Officer (CEO) appointments under the multiparty regime has seriously undermined civil servants' morale. Periodically the Ministry of Natural Resources, Energy and Environment takes an interest, but at grassroots level its threats to fine polluters appear toothless (*Daily Times*, 29 October 2009).

In some respects Ndirande – like the river that flows through it – is owned by no one. No one takes responsibility for its development or maintenance, though many claim to have authority over parts of it. But these complications are not inevitable. They were less acute during Malawi's first two or three decades of independent government. At that stage there were fewer layers of complexity and Kamuzu Banda's regime provided a clearer overall policy vision. Even today, in other parts of Malawi, there are local exceptions. Where there is in practice a strong centralising authority (such as a CEO in Kasungu town or a strong chieftaincy in Rumphi) that monitors performance and ensures compliance, as in Rwanda, coordination and better collaborative problem-solving can happen. But in the absence of idiosyncratic conditions such as these, collective action on the part of the authorities is weak and the effectiveness of public goods provision is severely constrained (Cammack and Kanyongolo 2010; Cammack 2012a: 18–22).

Unresolved policy conflicts in Niger As discussed in the last chapter, in Niger during the presidency of Tandja Mamadou (1999–2010), the purchase of ambulances – a part of the solution to a key bottleneck in the improvement of maternal mortality – was not joined up to other parts of the solution: the fuel, vehicle maintenance and staffing for emergency evacuation services. We also noted how primary health-care has been generally undermined by unresolved contradictions between two reforms of health-care financing.

Paralleling what happened in many other African countries, a policy of offering 'free' primary health-care to under-fives was adopted on a populist basis in 2006, without several of the preconditions for its success, including a budget. This was superimposed on top of a functioning cost-recovery system inspired by the Bamako Initiative. The cost-recovery arrangements have continued to operate in principle for the minority of patients not covered by other exemptions, but they have been seriously undermined. Health units have lost their only reliable source of non-salary funding. The result has been a significant weakening of provider incentives in the public sector, severe shortages of drugs at the primary level and a considerable expansion of de facto privatisation (Olivier de Sardan et al. 2010b: 2–3; Diarra 2011; Kafando et al. 2011; Olivier de Sardan 2012a).

These particular incidents are part of a wider pattern in which populist measures of infrastructure provision are delinked from, if not in direct conflict with, the resource planning of line ministries. This pattern does not just apply to the health area. In all areas of provision the state lacks credibility because of its inability to undertake policy measures in a sustained way. Sharp contrasts persist between announced intentions and the reality on the ground. Egged on by neoliberal thinking brought in by donors, the central state has largely withdrawn from public goods delivery in many sectors. From 2004, new elected municipal authorities created under the decentralisation reform were expected to take up the slack. However, decentralisation was implemented without real political backing. The funds that the state was committed to devolve to the districts were never disbursed. Consequently, local governments have remained understaffed and under-resourced. In some but not all areas, the gaps have been filled by NGOs, whose projects have become a favoured mode of organisation.

The end result of these intersecting changes has been that public goods delivery in Niger has been sporadic and patchy at best. It is influenced in any given locality by which bits of the state or the municipality happen to operate and how well positioned the community is to organise its own palliative measures. Joint projects exist but tend to end up suffering from coordination problems, with each actor protecting its own interests, autonomy and prerogatives.

First-level causes APPP findings converge with a wider literature in singling out the same pair of remarkably persistent and wider institutional factors as responsible for the problems described above. These two common features, which are documented and discussed in the literature, appear to account for the vast majority of the particular problems encountered:

- the superimposition of successive waves of public sector reform, often under donor influence, without sufficient efforts to resolve the inconsistencies thereby created; and
- populist policy initiatives, especially by presidents before and during election campaigns, without consultation with the affected sector planners (or donors) and without consideration of the resource implications.

The 'piling up' of donor-inspired institutional reforms is a long-established theme for several sub-regions of Africa.[3] The increasing popularity of populist, on-the-campaign-trail policy-making has also been a strong theme in recent work, although appreciations of it vary.[4] There are two things that have not, perhaps, had enough attention in these previous discussions. One is the degree to which these two elements are linked and mutually reinforcing. The other is whether they form a pattern that is strictly inevitable, as opposed to a choice that has been made by national leaders and their international partners, and which could be reversed. We shall come back to what this would take and why it has not happened, but only after giving some attention to the other type of institutional blockage to public goods provision that is of interest here, the weakness of what we have called politically enforced performance disciplines.

The politics of provider indiscipline

Again, what we found for health applies more broadly. Of course, difficulties in addressing key bottlenecks in provision in the study countries almost always involve general, and often extreme, resource shortages. However, our research uncovered many instances where these problems were compounded by weaknesses in either the allocation or the performance of the available human resources (technical and administrative staff). In many cases, unresolved problems in public provision could be connected directly with an absence of the

---

3 See Therkildsen (2000), Bierschenk and Olivier de Sardan (2003), Kayizzi-Mugerwa (2003), Batley and Larbi (2005) and Olivier de Sardan (2009b).

4 For example, Lawson and Rakner (2005), Cammack et al. (2007), van de Walle (2007), Fjeldstad and Therkildsen (2008), Hyden and Mmuya (2008) and Booth and Golooba-Mutebi (2009).

disciplines expected within any hierarchically ordered organisation: rules not being clearly laid down or enforced, instructions not being followed, vital jobs not being done, and so on.

When rules and regulations are clearly delineated and enforced, whether by state officials, community leaders or traditional authorities, it is common sense that the provision of public goods will be better than when they are not. Where rules are not backed by either credible sanctions or informal social pressures, individuals and groups will tend to behave in ways that are socially harmful. Our two sources of institutional blockage – incoherence and ill-discipline – obviously interact. On the one hand, it is harder to impose performance disciplines where mandates are unclear and policies contain serious internal and external inconsistencies. On the other hand, where providers are inadequately motivated to perform in their jobs, they are hardly likely to be driven to address problems that are outside their sphere of direct responsibility.

It is no surprise, of course, that we have found major problems of this sort. A substantial body of research now documents in precise detail the ways in which behaviour in public sector organisations, including service delivery organisations, fails to correspond to the officially expected pattern (Blundo et al. 2006; Blundo and Olivier de Sardan 2007). For some countries, this includes a convincing historical narrative of how things came to be that way (Anders 2001; Golooba-Mutebi 2007; Anders 2009; Becker 2009). These accounts portray a situation that is more complex than implied by the standard account of public sector deterioration underlying the original Washington Consensus (Olivier de Sardan 2008a; Crook 2010; Blundo 2011a, 2012). However, they reinforce the appreciation that outcomes for those at the receiving end of public goods provision are abysmal in most places most of the time, for reasons that have much to do with the breakdown of vertical disciplines.

APPP sought not just to add to this literature but to explore the previously neglected topic of whether and why there are exceptions and variations within the general picture. Two kinds of departure from the general pattern may be distinguished in principle. The first is what Crook (2010), Leonard (2010), Levy (2011) and Roll (2011) call 'islands' or 'pockets' of effectiveness within states that have weak governance – specific agencies or offices where, because of changes stopping short of outright privatisation, staff disciplines are maintained or enhanced in the face of the prevailing logics of behaviour within the public service at large. The second kind of departure from the general pattern involves variation between periods or across countries.

Pockets of effectiveness We found some examples of pockets of effectiveness. However, they involve something close to privatisation: the mandating of private associations of the trade union type to provide public goods alongside a paid private service.

The most interesting examples of pockets of effectiveness emerging from the APPP fieldwork concern a weak state's franchising of the management of transport stations, cattle markets and slaughterhouses to corporate bodies of a trade union or business association type. We have examples of this from Niger, Senegal and Sierra Leone (Gómez-Temesio 2010; Olivier de Sardan et al. 2010a: 26, 31; Workman 2011b; Cissokho 2012). In these cases, the management tasks performed involve the provision of public or collective goods relating to time schedules, security and hygiene.

The arrangements are, in part, the solution to a problem of collective action among the immediate participants, drivers or vehicle owners and meat producers. However, they are also a result of the state's delegation of key public goods functions, including policing and tax collection, to a non-state body. The institutional arrangements remain quite imperfect (still, in important respects, corrupt and faction-ridden) but display a relatively high degree of discipline and, therefore, effectiveness in much of what they do. In relation to tax collection, the examples are comparable with those provided by studies of 'associational taxation' in Ghana and elsewhere (Joshi and Ayee 2008).

Variation between periods or across countries The APPP findings on variation between periods and across countries bring us back to the theme with which we concluded Chapter 3, the differences among subtypes of neopatrimonial political regime.[5] Across countries and periods, we have a predictably abundant crop of examples of highly clientelistic forms of political rule that, in practice, undermine the ability of the public administration to perform as it is 'supposed' to. On the other hand, from one current case (Rwanda) and from

---

5 We discussed the core meaning of this concept at the beginning of Chapter 2.

the whole span of post-independence experience in other countries (Côte d'Ivoire, Kenya, Malawi, Tanzania, Uganda, etc.), we know that clientelistic undermining of bureaucratic functioning is a variable and not an unavoidable given. Furthermore, the secondary literature on Africa and Asia agrees with our own country studies in suggesting that where bureaucracies function relatively well in public goods provision, this is not necessarily because neopatrimonial logics of behaviour are absent from the national political system (Future State 2010; Kelsall et al. 2010; Henley and van Donge 2012).

As we have seen, APPP studies and other research in Niger by LASDEL have generated a particularly rich account of the way clientelistic appointments prevent a rational allocation of human resources in the health sector, and the enforcement of even minimal standards of performance. Because some of its key transitions are relatively recent, Malawi provides a second good source of examples of differences across regimes and time periods. The two presidential terms of Bakili Muluzi, which coincided with the advent of multi-party politics, provide a stark example of the breakdown of vertical disciplines under the impact of a new form of clientelistic political competition in a winner-takes-all electoral system. The preceding regime of Kamuzu Banda was a contrasting type of neopatrimonial regime, in a single-party context. Finally, the recently deceased president, Bingu wa Mutharika, assumed a political style in his first term in which vertical disciplines were restored somewhat, in a context that remained politically competitive and clientelistic. In his second term, however, and under a different set of political constraints and opportunities, both political and bureaucratic corruption returned to centre stage, and civil service morale deteriorated once again (Cammack 2012a: 52; 2012b).

One of the routes by which the style of political leadership at the top impacts on the way the civil service functions in Malawi is through the 'tall-poppy syndrome'. This expression – also called 'hedge clipping' – refers to the phenomenon in public bureaucracies where unusually competent or hard-working individuals are regularly 'cut down' by colleagues. Reflecting the zero-sum outlook 'where you benefit, I suffer' (Mills and Herbst 2012: 232), this form of jealousy (*nsanje* in Chichewa) obviously hinders efficient joint working. The extent to which its harmful effects on performance are realised is determined by, among other things, the extent to which vertical disciplines are enforced. Insiders say that hedge clipping has been increasingly prevalent since Malawi's democratic transition (Booth et al. 2006).

The Malawi example confirms in this way that some kinds of neopatrimonial presidential system utterly undermine the discipline of the public bureaucracy, including the lower tiers of the hierarchy. By contrast, without ceasing to be fundamentally neopatrimonial, some historical regimes, such as Kamuzu Banda's, allocate patronage in ways that do not destroy bureaucratic disciplines. In such instances, it is not necessary for authority to be rule-bound, and the bureaucrats do not need to be highly trained, appointed purely on merit, well remunerated or (in the jargon) well 'facilitated' – although all of those help. The most important ingredient is political drive (Cammack and Kelsall 2010).

Democracy: help or hindrance?

The suggestion that both policy coherence and bureaucratic effectiveness have been achieved under *some* regimes of a broadly neopatrimonial type raises rather pointedly the issue of 'democracy'. According to the standard 'demand-side' version of the principal–agent approach to development problems, democracy is the solution to problems such as those that we have been discussing. To what extent is this borne out by the evidence of our country studies?

To ask this question is not to advance any hypothesis about the general superiority of bureaucratic or authoritarian regimes or forms of accountability over the democratic kind. In general, dictatorships have a poor record in public goods delivery. On occasion, such as under the military intervention of 2010 in Niger, appointed administrators have done a good job of dealing with problems that had defeated the former, elected, local authorities. However, the reasons are to be found in the particular circumstances, not in any intrinsic advantage (Olivier de Sardan 2012b: 7–9).

This caveat notwithstanding, the APPP fieldwork has added to the evidence that, in its *current* form and under prevailing conditions, African democracy is, at best, a weak source of pressure for performance if top-down disciplines are absent. At worst, it has encouraged politicians to intensify their enjoyment of the spoils of office – through personal appropriation of rents of various kinds – which has served in turn to legitimise rule-breaking by officials and to excuse the non-enforcement of rules from top to bottom of government. This applies not just to national politics but no less to situations where multiparty competition has been introduced at the local level.

The repeated postponement of local government (district/city) elections in Malawi since 2005 has meant that there has been no basis for forming a judgement on the ability of *local* democracy to make a difference to the issues of policy incoherence and provider indiscipline. In the absence of elected assemblies/councils, District Commissioners and city CEOs select members of ad hoc committees to advise them. Many city authorities admit they prefer operating without local councillors – who are supposed to pass bylaws, raise revenues, debate policies and oversee district/city accounts. Poor residents say they miss having councillors because they served (2000–05) as their conduit to government. This should not necessarily be interpreted as a statement about bottom-up accountability or public goods. However, it does mean that the evidence on the potential benefits of democratic decentralisation in Malawi is currently rather inconclusive.

That is not the case in Uganda. There too advocates of decentralisation tend to assume that ordinary people have the capacity to influence decision-making if it occurs locally. However, the best research on sub-national processes in Uganda (e.g. Golooba-Mutebi 2005: 165) has always questioned this assumption. Not only are people often illiterate and lacking in basic information, but their potential leverage is weakened by the nature of politics. The winning of local elections is more a matter of buying the support of the right people than a matter of the candidates' personal qualities or their parties' platforms. Leaders who have bought their way to positions of power may have debts to repay, but the beneficiaries are unlikely to be the generality of ordinary voters. As a result, voters come to see the delivery of public goods as a privilege, not a right (Golooba-Mutebi 2008; Ssebunya 2010: 24).

Calling to mind the opinion among Malawians that since 1994 there has been 'too much freedom', APPP researchers in Uganda tell us that 'for many rural dwellers in Uganda, democratic processes seem to mean freedom from civic obligations. This has detrimental effects on collective action efforts and the enforcement of laws to facilitate them' (Ssebunya 2010: 30). The introduction of downward accountabilities in the form of local competitive elections appears to provide only a poor substitute for top-down disciplines. Elections can also weaken the ability of officials to provide the sort of public goods that mitigate the negative externalities associated with uncontrolled behaviour by individuals or households. These include formulating and enforcing rules or conducting public education campaigns to prevent outbreaks of disease or environmental disasters. Specifically, Uganda's District Council Chairmen and the civil servants who report to them are, in general, reluctant to enforce bylaws that are unpopular with the population, because they expect this will lose them votes (ibid.: 15, 16).

The relationship between democratisation and economic development is a notoriously tricky issue. In presenting the findings of APPP research, we have tried, not always successfully, to avoid a simple for-and-against debate in which empirically grounded statements about the limitations of existing multiparty political systems are seen as attacks on the idea of democracy. However, one thing on which all comers ought to be able to agree is that the institutions of formal democracy do not work in a vacuum. Their functioning is always shaped by the social and economic context.

Democracy in context A 'Joint Statement' issued by five research programmes including APPP in April 2012 stated:

> Clientelism in Africa is to a greater or lesser extent competitive under both authoritarian and more democratic regimes. Political elites are fragmented along economic, regional, ethnic, religious and other lines. Cooperation for the greater good is extremely difficult, so different members of the elite compete with each other to build and sustain winning coalitions. They do so by allocating private benefits to those groups on whose support they rely and targeting threats at significant opponents. Typically, multi-party elections formalise and sharpen this competition with often mixed results for development. (APPP et al. 2012: 9)

From the point of view of the standard advice on good governance, this last aspect is a paradox. Democracy is supposed to be the solution. It is supposed to be the means by which citizens make governments respond to their will and become accountable. In reality, the relationships observed on the ground correspond only in limited and problematic ways to this ideal.

In political science, studies of the causal relationships between democracy as measured by standard indicators and outcomes, such as economic growth rates or human development indices, have been taken as far as they can go. While the findings exclude extreme views such as those that imply an incompatibility between electoral democracy and economic progress in poor countries, they are otherwise inconclusive and raise new issues (Doucouliagos and Ulubasoglu 2008; Rocha Menocal 2011). The inference, even from books dedicated to establishing the advantages of democracy (e.g. Halperin et al. 2010: ch. 2), is that there are core issues that cut across the formal characteristics of regimes, and that these are the issues that matter most when it comes to the governance of economic transformation and public goods provision. In other words, the focus now needs to be on particular variable features of broadly democratic systems and how these co-evolve with other variables in particular cases over periods of time (Gerring et al. 2011).

The trouble with democracy, as a substantive reality and not just a set of formal arrangements, is that its effectiveness depends on social and economic conditions that are not yet enjoyed in most developing countries. Competitive elections, checks and balances, and other elements of the typical liberal democratic constitution, have undoubted advantages if they can be made to work. However, the evidence is clear that the formal arrangements of liberal democracy have radically different effects in different kinds of social and economic context. History teaches that some sequences are feasible and others not, because the economic, social and political dimensions of human progress are interdependent. More specifically, the evidence tends to support Brett's (2012) thesis that open democratic processes have only ever been established in countries that have strong states, cohesive societies and liberal capitalist economies.

It is vital to be realistic about how to promote and support democracy in at least two ways. The first has been a dominant theme in the work of the Crisis States Centre at the London School of Economics among others. Careless promotion of elections and economic liberalisation – the trappings of democracy and capitalism – in countries where inter-communal relations and political settlements are fragile can be very costly in terms of violence and human life (Kaplan 2008; Lindemann 2008; Auteserre 2010; Putzel 2010). Secondly, even if this danger can be overcome or does not apply, many young democracies are not particularly developmental. And we know from both theory and empirical case research why this is the case.

Democracy works, when it works, by producing a battle of ideas between contending parties about what to do in the public realm. This is often messy and produces socially useful outcomes only after much contestation and trial and error – contrary to notions like 'democratic ownership' in development planning (Faust 2010). In African settings, clientelism (vote-buying in its various forms) is a much cheaper and more reliable option for power-hungry politicians seeking support than promises to improve policies for the delivery of public goods (Collier 2007: 44–50). What wins elections is not sound development planning but a popular public policy gesture or two accompanied by targeted handouts to particular key clients and voters in swing constituencies (Whitfield 2011b). Under such conditions, politics typically generates policies that are the opposite of those required for successful economic transformation (Leftwich 2000).

One reason for the persistence of this pattern is that, until economies and societies have substantial organisational capacity, it is genuinely hard to deliver on promises to improve the provision of public goods. It is not surprising, therefore, that politicians throughout history have shied away from campaigning on such a basis, usually preferring the clientelistic option (North et al. 2009). The only significant exception is where a policy gesture is judged to be cheap and risk-free – such as abolishing a tax or charge in the confidence that donors or the next incumbent will pick up the bill (Kjaer and Therkildsen 2011; Poulton 2011). Where more coherent and consequential policy action is concerned, coordination challenges and risks are not the only deterrent. There is also a collective action problem proper, in that any individual politician who considers such action will be put off by the likelihood of free-riding on any benefits by other members of the political class (Geddes 1994).

Voters, for their part, rarely have any evidence of the actual provision of public goods by politicians, so any such promises are not considered credible. They too, therefore, opt for targeted benefits, believing on the basis of experience, that 'their' candidate will channel these to them (Keefer and Khemani 2005; Keefer 2007). That often means opting for the candidate with the right ethnic or regional credentials, even if the voter attaches little importance to ethnicity in other contexts (Posner 2005).

Anyway, within neopatrimonial democracies ordinary people have ways of solving their everyday problems that have nothing to do with voting in elections. In these systems, patronage networks reach all the way down to local communities. People are attuned to the way such networks work, and use them for their own benefit. Some people access goods through networks based on ethnicity, origin, family ties or party affiliation. In many cases, the results are more constant and reliable than state provision. Symbiotic relations are created between leaders and followers in which the latter turn a blind eye to leaders 'eating' from public resources so long as some of the crumbs from the table are shared.

The result is that citizens and leaders operate according to (at least) two registers – one formal, using the language of democracy and good governance, and the other more informal but strongly embedded. Together, they use either or a mixture of both in seeking to meet their respective needs.

Democracy and collective action It follows from this discussion of democracy that politicians who might have a personal inclination to stake their careers and reputations on addressing the big challenges of national development – such as building an efficient road network to support smallholder farmers – will be triply discouraged from doing so. They will be intimidated first by the sheer difficulty of doing so, given the current capabilities of the state and the national private sector; secondly by an unfavourable calculus of political costs and benefits, including the political version of the free-rider problem; and thirdly by the expectation that voters are unlikely to believe their promises.

Of course, social movements that translate into political movements around programmatic issues have occurred on occasion in parts of Latin America and South Asia (Future State 2005; Gaventa and McGee 2010). However, in most African countries, including all of those studied by APPP, ordinary citizens face prohibitive collective problems from the outset because of their geographical dispersion and social fragmentation, as pointed out by Bates in relation to agriculture thirty years ago (1981). People face a host of social dilemmas that inhibit their ability to organise and act together. These are rooted in 'informational' and 'motivational' problems that, even in richer societies, hinder the mobilisation of large groups, the formulation of common demands and the ability to hold others including leaders to account (Corduneanu-Huci et al. 2013: 79–98). Social and ethnic heterogeneity amplify these effects. Even political parties have difficulty articulating common interests or organising nationwide collective action. Parties are largely vehicles for individual political leaders and their networks.

We return to factors inhibiting collective action in Chapter 5. But first we need to say more about how political competition in a clientelistic system reduces the possibility of 'demand' for better public performance emerging from the bottom up. Malawi provides a good example of the general phenomenon. Although flavoured by some of the country's particular history, the Malawi experience illustrates well the logic that applies when the spoils of political office provide by far the most enticing avenue of advancement for members of a national elite.

Single-party mentalities in a multiparty setting

Malawi has experienced two electorally endorsed changes of president since its transition from Kamuzu Banda's regime in 1994. To this extent it may be said to have a multiparty system. However, not only are parties almost entirely personal vehicles, but incumbent presidents have overwhelming power to build parties around themselves by buying off the parliamentarians on the losing side and, in spite of constitutional provisions to the contrary, bringing them over to share in the benefits of office. This is good for political stability, but extremely bad for the development of programmatic political competition, not to mention the consolidation of parliament as either a representative body or as a factor in a division of powers (Rakner and van de Walle 2009).

The exceptional power of incumbents does not, of course, eliminate the risk of losing the next election, especially if there are presidential term limits. Incumbents, therefore, do all they can to consolidate their hold on power, including extending the control exercised by their party or clientelist network on the associational life of the country down to the lowest possible level. As a result, the idea that incumbent parties are bound to capture and control grassroots social and self-help activities remains a central feature of the political culture in Malawi. According to the APPP fieldwork, it represents a significant barrier to genuine collective action for development in several parts of the country (Cammack and Kanyongolo 2010; Cammack 2012a). This is best exemplified by the public water outlets ('kiosks') and the market committees in the Ndirande neighbourhood of Blantyre.

Political capture of water points After the 1994 transition, there were
new waves of migration from the rural areas to Malawi's towns and
cities. As the urban population grew, the old piped-water infrastructure
in Ndirande – owned and managed by the Blantyre Water Board
(BWB) – was no longer up to the task. NGOs and donor-funded
projects stepped in, constructing new public water kiosks which were
to be managed and operated by local water committees.

They – like the voluntary health, education and community-policing
committees that were popular at the same time – were seen by government, donors and NGOs as elements of a new participatory local
democracy linked to decentralisation (Cammack et al. 2007). But,
prior to the transition, the ruling Malawi Congress Party (MCP) –
through its constituency chairmen, and women and youth committees
– had dominated most public efforts and community projects. Well
entrenched in Malawians' minds, then, was the notion that political
parties start and lead initiatives. Therefore, the new water facilities
were seen locally as initiatives of Muluzi's United Democratic Front
(UDF) party, a view the ruling party was happy to encourage. Soon
after the kiosks were constructed, local leaders of the UDF took over
management of many of them as chairmen of water committees. Some
had new kiosks built on their plots, and employed their family members
as water sellers. Water profits were split between the BWB and the
UDF members, leading to multimillion-kwacha arrears to the Board.

In 2005, the new president, Bingu wa Mutharika, abandoned the
UDF and formed his own Democratic Progressive Party (DPP). As
soon as that party's local structures were strong enough, they (with
the help of the police) wrested control of the kiosks in Ndirande
from the UDF. But the UDF people made off with the accumulated
funds, leading the Water Board to cut off the water supply. The
upshot, at the time of the 2009 fieldwork, was that few kiosks were
still operational. Many residents had reverted to using unsafe water
sources (Cammack and Kanyongolo 2010: 30–2).

Belatedly, the government's new National Water Policy (Government of Malawi 2005) established Water Users' Associations (WUAs),
aiming to place management of outlets in the hands of community
groups formed by the water users themselves. One of the intentions
was to depoliticise water services. However, the initiative has run
into complicated local disputes reflecting similar expectations about
political control. These were unresolved as of early 2012 (Cammack

2012a: 11–17). Government had failed dismally to transfer 'owner-ship' to citizens or to deliver cheap, plentiful water in central areas of Ndirande.

Water provision in Ndirande – like many other activities in Malawi – has become a rent-earning, vote-winning service, captured by poli-ticians and the elite, with few of the attributes of a well-managed public good. This hinders people's access to available water, deepening the effects of the attributes of the community discussed in the next chapter and exacerbating the problems caused by the poor state of the infrastructure.

Politics and market management In the 1970s the old market in Ndirande was moved to its current location – a large open field next to the Nasolo river. Originally, the central market was managed by the city, and vendors paid market fees that covered the upkeep of the toilets and public areas. Water was supplied free of charge. There was a vendors' market committee affiliated to the ruling MCP. With the advent of multipartyism, a new committee – led by UDF members – was elected by vendors. After the DPP was formed in 2005, the city decided it preferred working with ruling-party-affiliated market committees throughout Blantyre, and appointed a DPP member to head up a new committee in the Ndirande market. After that vendors were divided in their allegiance to the UDF and the DPP committees.

In this situation 'the market master – a city employee – has a fine line to walk between what the city perceives to be the legitimate committee and what the vendors feel is representative of their interests ... because it was elected by them' (Cammack and Kanyongolo 2010: 34). In 2010, the leaders of the two committees agreed a truce, but a new layer of politicisation and complex mis-coordination was introduced when an independent politician was elected as the local MP and some vendors thought they should start a new committee loyal to her (Cammack 2012a: 22–7).

In late 2008, Ndirande market caught fire and a large portion of it was destroyed. Many of the vendors moved out on to the streets. Because this happened shortly before the national elections, money was promised by various politicians, including former president Muluzi and the then president Mutharika. The city raised funds to rebuild the market, promising to have the work completed by the middle of 2010 (*Weekend Nation*, 20 June 2009). Two years later, however, the market was still under construction. There was only one working water tap – which was not functioning at all for some months in 2010/11 – and one latrine without running water. The wall between the market and the clinic was the informally designated toilet. Vendors had dug holes near their benches to reach water of dubious quality, which they shared among themselves and sold to strangers. City cleaners were attempting to do their job without sufficient chemicals, tools or gloves. The road outside the market was badly potholed and overflowing skips were not emptied for days.

The reasons underlying this dismal situation are not unlike the issues surrounding water provision. First, market management is badly organised, with different lines of reporting to various city departments and the poor coordination that follows from that. For instance, market and toilet fees – collected by ticket sellers working under the market master – end up in the city's finance department along with city rates. Licence fees collected by HSAs from shops, restaurants, hairdressers and the like, on the other hand, go to the city's health and sanitation department. Market cleaners and their supplies come from the health department budget, while repairs to market infrastructure are the responsibility of the engineering department. Security guards are privately employed, though paid with city funds. As one city official noted, 'this is not a good arrangement', as many staff do not report directly to the market master, but to different officials at the city's offices. 'This slows responses and it takes a long time to get some things done' (interview of 25 March 2011, cited in Cammack 2012a: 25–6). These multiple lines of responsibility and reporting also make it harder for market users or vendors to know how to interact with the authorities about specific issues.

Secondly, because the vendors and their representative committees are divided along party political lines, they are unable to present a united front to demand that the city consistently performs tasks that would improve the market. While they often refuse to pay daily market fees (K50 in 2009) to show their displeasure with the delay in reconstruction, that is hardly an effective strategy for getting the city to speed up rebuilding. The vendors' shifting divisions are, of course, exacerbated by city administrators who, to please their political masters, have on occasion set aside vendors' elected representatives and worked with those (whom they appoint) who belong to the ruling party.

Kamuzu Banda's legacies and the logic of competitive clientelism Dr Kamuzu Banda's MCP party ruled for thirty years and little went on in the country without its leaders being involved. In those years, Malawians became used to being represented by political-party officials. In addition, for centuries they have been governed by chiefs, whose authority has waxed and waned, but who have always remained involved with local development. Today it is normal for chiefs and the party elite to initiate and manage programmes, interact with state bureaucracies and funders on issues of development, organise and oversee community committees, and act as the conduit for information passed between leaders and citizens. Furthermore, chiefs and their *nduna* (advisers), and MPs and constituency-level party leaders, are expected by ordinary Malawians to deliver goods to their own communities, while it is the president who is meant to take care of the nation as a whole.

It is not perceived to be unusual, therefore, that local leaders capture what are legally public goods (including food aid or agricultural subsidies as well as water kiosks) and transform them into 'club goods' delivered to their own people, especially to ardent loyalists. It is also understood that, when a leader loses power, his loyalists must give way to a new leader and his clients, who will then take their turn to 'eat'. During such transitions it is not unusual to hear old clients bemoan the fact that the new ruling party's members have taken over 'their' infrastructure, which was built by 'their leader'. 'Have your leader build your own', new clients are told by members of defunct ruling parties.

Such reasoning – what might be thought of as a single-party mentality in a multiparty setting – tends to divide communities. It encourages people to look to politicians for access to goods, hoping that their patron and party will win elections and gain access to state resources. This is the underside of the clientelist relations that characterise the type of neopatrimonial state that prevails in Malawi. Since chiefs also funnel development aid to their jurisdictions, they also deliver to 'their own people' and not other chiefs' villagers. The fact that state authorities do not provide much directly, and are largely absent on the ground, reinforces the view that it is wiser to cosy up to locally rooted chiefs and politicians and do their bidding than to follow the advice that trickles down from donors to make 'demands' on state agents who generally do not deliver.

This situation can be written off as a failure, a measure of the distance between Malawian practice and liberal-democratic norms. However, it is more realistic and more practical to regard it as a problem of both local- and elite-level collective action in search of a solution. Current political practice is not just a legacy of the past. It reflects, among other things, the fact that elite Malawians have access to few business or professional occupations that are materially as rewarding as politics. Parliamentarians who are not on the government side are well compensated by local standards but they profit less than those participating in the spoils of governmental office. Democracy does not work as it does under the watchful eye of a capitalist middle class because Malawi does not have a capitalist economy.

So long as that is the case, arrangements are needed that allow some sharing of political spoils. Arguably, the challenge for Malawians is to find ways of doing that which is at least marginally less harmful to the quality of policy-making and the delivery of public goods, so that processes of development and transformation can begin in earnest.

Summing up

Many of the immediate causes of low standards and persistent bottlenecks across different fields of public goods provision in our countries of interest have to do with some combination of policy-driven institutional incoherence and poor vertical disciplines. It is conventional to see the solutions in principal–agent terms, as a matter of getting service providers to do what political leaders and voters want them to do. But that is unrealistic. It is a mistake to believe that 'democracy', taken as centring on more frequent and cleaner elections, is going to be a reliable way to get better public policies in Africa in the near future. The more efficient electoral processes are, the more effectively they will transmit the incentive effects that make politicians short-termist and clientelistic. Voters are complicit in this. It makes no more sense to treat voters as development principals – committed to 'calling political leaders to account' – than to treat leaders, in competitive clientelistic systems, as their agents.

From APPP and other research, we know that this does not just apply to Malawi, Niger and Uganda. It is relevant even, and in some ways most clearly, to the African country that is generally considered to have made most headway in consolidating multiparty politics and political liberalism, Ghana. There too political competition centres on the allocation of discretionary benefits, not on the delivery of the risky, slow-payoff, support to public goods and private investment that the country needs (Lindberg 2009; Hyden 2010; Whitfield 2011b, 2011a). It also applies to Tanzania, the country whose dominant political party might seem to have offered a suitable framework for solving elite collective action barriers to the addressing of major national issues, but where elite fragmentation has assumed the form of acute inner-party factionalism (Cooksey and Kelsall 2011; Therkildsen 2012; Therkildsen and Bourgouin 2012). The situation is similar in Uganda (Kjaer and Katusiimeh 2012) and several degrees worse, but not different in kind, in Tanzania's large neighbour, the DRC (Keefer and Wolters 2011).

This is bad news for the structural transformation and the provision of the basic public goods that development requires. That in turn is bad news for democracy and political freedom. For without economic transformation and better social provision, a genuine democratic deepening will stay off the agenda of the poorest countries for many years to come. If, as we agree, solutions to the problem of governance for economic transformation have to be relevant to countries that have multiparty systems and consider themselves democracies, then we have to be able to say how the consequences of elite fragmentation for developmentally significant collective action might also be mitigated in the context of multiparty political systems.

This is the fundamental question that needs to be answered if better advice than 'first get good governance' is to be given to African governance reformers and their allies. It is the unavoidable issue for any operationalisation of 'good fit' governance for contemporary Africa. The elite-level collective action problems blocking effective support to economic transformation *may* be insuperable under current conditions in Africa. In principle, however, problems of collective action are solvable if the right institutions can be created, and history – particularly in Asia – provides many examples of progressive political change under conditions not unlike those of contemporary Africa.

5 | THE SPACE FOR LOCAL PROBLEM-SOLVING AND PRACTICAL HYBRIDITY

In Chapter 4, we saw that barriers to effective public goods delivery are often related to multilevel collective action problems, from the national political level downwards. Here we address the more specific issue of local (sub-national) action to address problems such as those created by policy incoherence and provider indiscipline. Readers will recall that the enabling environment for such local remedial action emerged as a third type of important institutional variation in the APPP case studies of public goods provision.

As noted in Chapter 1, it is well established – thanks to Ostrom and others – that the ability of groups of individuals to overcome classic collective action dilemmas varies considerably from situation to situation. The various dimensions of context that matter include the presence or absence of social, economic or political factors that fragment, misinform and demotivate communities, and inhibit collective action.

We now argue that it is vital that outsiders take these limitations as a given when designing development interventions, especially in Africa, where fragmentation, heterogeneity, poor information-sharing and perverse incentives are ubiquitous in almost all countries. Institutional initiatives that address these problems – which may mean building upon locally recognised ways of doing things – are more likely to succeed than those making assumptions of the principal–agent type. We go on to show that aid-funded interventions can very easily divert or inhibit collective action of the self-help variety, either because of the direct effects of cash injections or because of the imposition of inappropriate models of organisation. Finally, we draw attention to the variable willingness of governmental authorities to tolerate sub-national initiatives, where stakeholders happen to succeed in coming together to address a specific blockage in public goods provision.

Solving problems locally

The concept of collective action that we are advancing in this book is not limited to any particular level of social engagement. There are in fact good reasons for seeing the elite-level action issues pinpointed in earlier chapters as the most fundamental development issue for most African countries. We return to that theme in our Conclusion. However, as we began to discuss in Chapter 3 in the maternal health context, experience shows that there is a place for specifically local, meaning sub-national, problem-solving. At this level, we believe, it is vital that solutions are locally anchored. What do we mean by that?

Context matters Local anchorage implies two things, and it is worth distinguishing them. One is the simple proposition that successful institutions of local collective action are those that address the specific obstacles that are relevant locally. This might appear almost tautological but for the fact that it is common, and even normal, that the institutions applied to local problems employ generic formulas that are not tailored to the actual context – that is, to the actors in the situation, the extent and nature of the free-rider problem, the strengths and limits of existing ways of doing things, and the alliances and other resources that may be available.

Shivakumar (2005: 105) sums up the general view of the Ostrom school on this point in this way:

> Development is always a local phenomenon, where local refers to the relevant problem area. Human development and economic progress are rooted in the enhanced ability of individuals – brought together within specific contexts and in light of some encountered collective action problem – to adapt by developing the institutional contexts needed to deal with their situation. To be effective, therefore, institutions must refer to a particular context of a collective action problem and may ramify to other domains.

Consequently, devising solutions without local knowledge is likely to be unhelpful.

Here we have one element for a concept of what it means for an institution to be 'locally anchored': the extent to which it involves behaviours that are, consciously or otherwise, problem-solving *in the context*. The other concerns the aspect of drawing on previous experience or making use of institutional elements that have been employed locally in the past. Shivakumar alludes to this when he writes: '[T]he future of effective development through good government does not lie in coaxing particular constitutional models to work in transplanted settings ... [I]t depends instead [on] advancing systems of interaction ... that simultaneously draw strength from and build upon prevailing institutional understandings' (ibid.: 66). However, Shivakumar's formulation 'drawing strength from prevailing understandings' remains a little too metaphorical. Can we do better? Further evidence and analysis from APPP says we can.

If there is a genuinely universal truth about governance for transformation, it is that pre-existing institutions need to be treated as a potential resource for reforms that improve development outcomes, not swept aside in a hurry to innovate. Successful institutions draw on the popular concepts of what is right and proper that are contained in local cultural 'repertoires'. Typically, however, they do so in a way that requires adaptation by, but not the supplanting of, the practices and standards of the modern state. They are practical hybrids. In APPP, we arrived at this notion through research in a number of fields designed to explore an initial working hypothesis about favouring institutions that 'work with the grain' of African societies. Here is a brief explanation of how our thinking evolved.

The notion of practical hybridity In an early contribution to APPP's discussion of the possible meaning of 'working with the grain', Tim Kelsall (2008b) provided a strong literature-based argument for recognising a limited number of long-term continuities in African social and political life. Drawing on his own fieldwork and other studies (Kelsall 2004; Kelsall et al. 2005; Kelsall 2008a, 2009), he argued that development efforts need to pay more serious attention to ways of harnessing the notions of moral and social obligation and interpersonal accountability that are among these elements of continuity. Since even today these notions tend to be bound up with ethnic, familial or religious social identities, it is likely that self-help efforts that build on shared identities or pre-existing organisational templates will be more successful than those that do not.

Of course, it is important not to overstate the homogeneity of values and norms across and within African societies and organisations. It is easy to exaggerate the extent to which people's actual behaviour corresponds to the 'traditions' they espouse formally (Olivier de Sardan 2008b). However, taking this warning seriously does not entail dismissing the whole idea of cultural commonalities, or indeed the importance of ethnicity.[1] We certainly need a different view of culture and cultural explanation than the one espoused by the anthropological functionalism and sociological modernisation theory of the twentieth century. Such a view may be found in Olivier de Sardan's account of the moral economy of corruption in Africa (1999) and in another form in Kelsall's (2009) contribution about what is left unexplained by game theory and social-mechanism concepts. The thesis of Chabal and Daloz (2006), in which culture refers more to shared systems of meaning than to 'values', is also helpful.

But perhaps the most direct assistance to theorising the APPP concept of practical hybridity is that provided some time ago by Swidler (1986). Swidler argues that the causal role of culture lies 'not in defining ends of action, but in providing cultural components that are used to construct strategies of action'. Therefore, culture does shape action, but only in the sense that 'the cultural repertoire limits the available range of strategies of action' (ibid.: 273, 284).

This view of the role of culture is consistent with the demands of empirical rigour. What 'resources' are suitable for adoption from the repertoire inherited from the past depends on what is in that repertoire and the particular action choices that are being made. These are all things that have to be investigated (for example, with a separate survey, as in the study of attitudes to local justice in Ghana summarised farther on). But Swidler also helps to answer the question: why should new institutions be stronger and more effective when they adopt elements of the local culture, hybridising them with elements drawn from the resources and traditions of the state?

Swidler's answer is both simple and practical. At least in settled periods, culture is drawn upon 'because of the high costs of cultural retooling to adopt new patterns of action' (ibid.: 284). In other words, it is too costly in social terms to invent all parts of a new

---

1 There is evidence that collective action for the provision of public goods is easier in communities where ethnic or some other identity is shared (Miguel 2004; Miguel and Gugerty 2005). At the same time, there seem to be ways to explain this that do not involve the hypothesis of a strong moral commitment to the group or that individual behaviour is typically value-driven (Habyarimana et al. 2007; Habyarimana et al. 2009; Kelsall 2009).

institution from scratch, so successful innovations tend to draw on elements inherited from the past. A more elaborated argument of the same type is found in Greif's (2006) historical study of institutional change in early modern Italy, where it is expressed in terms of game theory.

Drawing on Swidler in this way to elaborate the findings of Ostrom and Shivakumar, we may summarise our conceptual position as follows. The provision of some types of public goods will be enhanced by institutions that are locally anchored, in two senses. First, they will be problem-solving, in a collective action sense, in the relevant context. Secondly, they will be hybrids that make some use of local cultural repertoires.

Barriers to local problem-solving APPP research suggests that local problem-solving (e.g. to address the effects of policy incoherence or weak provider incentives) is by no means dead in local areas of rural and peri-urban Africa. Locally anchored institutions are not absent either. However, the space for both is more limited than might be expected. The reasons have to do with the national-level political factors discussed in Chapter 4, but also with a set of more specific factors. These include:

- difficulties of collective action – and thus the impossibility of the behaviours expected by principal–agent frameworks – caused by social fragmentation and lack of trust;
- distortions caused by the availability of donor money and foreign organisational templates, now delivered to the remotest rural areas by local governments and NGOs; and
- mechanical application of donor-inspired policy guidelines by sector ministries, such that local actors are prevented from coming together to provide their own solutions.

This chapter presents the evidence that supports these claims. First, we suggest why collective action of the self-help type among local actors is difficult in typical African environments, drawing examples mainly from experience in Malawi. We go on to explore the reasons why successful initiatives seem likely to draw institutional ingredients from different sources, combining them in 'practical hybrid' forms. The illustrations come from Malawi, Tanzania, Ghana and other parts of West Africa. Finally, we return to experiences in Niger and the various ways in which governments, the aid business and NGOs restrict the space for local problem-solving.

Collective action challenges in peri-urban Malawi

Local actors in the field situations studied by APPP teams face multiple problems of collective action. Peri-urban Malawi has some special features but illustrates many issues that are widely observed elsewhere. Ndirande is an extreme case in several respects. Other areas of Malawi, such as those included in the first phase of APPP research, provide more examples of successful local problem-solving than we found in Ndirande. In Rumphi town in the north, for instance, residents – including chiefs, local NGOs, vendors and business people – joined together to establish a city-centre sanitation project that lasted for some time. In Kasungu in central Malawi a combination of city officials, vendors, residents and the police established a police unit at the bus-station-cum-market that has continued to improve security. Some Water Users' Associations in some peri-urban settings – such as nearby Kachere – provide better service than in Ndirande. In other words, there are cases where Malawians manage to solve their social dilemmas and utilise their common-pool resources relatively well. But there are many cases where they do not, and Ndirande is a place where failure is the norm and therefore any successes are of special interest.

Fragmentation and mistrust Community members in Ndirande face difficulties in organising even the most elementary forms of self-help. This is for several, mutually reinforcing, reasons. To begin with, poverty makes it hard for people to work together to solve collective problems. Looking for work and eking out a precarious living take a great deal of time and energy, leaving little to spare. Few people anyway have skills or experience in organising community action. Many are ill educated and some are illiterate and innumerate. Many Malawians of all social classes tend to make sense of unexplained events by reference to witchcraft rather than science.

In addition, in places like Ndirande, the residents are 'translocal' (their livelihoods require them to move between towns and farms). Being translocal they are less motivated than they might be to improve their places of urban residence; 'home' is still in the countryside. Being transient, and tenants rather than homeowners, also gives rise to a more careless attitude about property and neighbourhood welfare. Newcomers are anyway less clued up on how things work in their communities, and how to effect change.[2] Many peri-urban residents are youthful too, with an interest in many more enticing activities than organising or joining groups to improve public services.

Other factors also divide communities and make it harder for them to identify with, trust or cooperate with people they do not know well. The fear of being bewitched is widespread, and affects behaviour in many sectors. As noted in Chapter 3, some women will not attend hospitals to deliver for fear their foetuses will somehow be snatched by witches. Residents will not complain to others about their antisocial behaviour (e.g. dumping rubbish) for fear they may hex them. People are especially fearful of strangers whose customs they do not fully understand, and whose backgrounds and reputations they do not know. This is a particular issue in a place like Ndirande, to where people migrate from all over the country (and beyond).

In spite of these constraints, in Ndirande there are a number of small face-to-face cooperative arrangements based on some kind of shared identity. They include *chipereganyu* savings clubs, where, say, a few market vendors pool small amounts of money, and the funds are given out each day to a different member of the group. Some of these clubs may aspire to become burial societies and loan associations. However, members' innumeracy, their paucity of organisational skills and mutual suspicion easily pull even these apart. Collective action that goes beyond the confines of these groups is quite rare. The creation of citizen groups that 'bridge' to more distant groups and are effective over the long term requires organising skills, capacities to communicate over distances, getting to know strangers and learning to trust them, all of which are in short supply or alien to them.

The kinds of public or collective goods that could be generated by self-help actions are, as a result, severely under-provided. For example, collective action by residents of the informal settlement of Ndirande to address serious health hazards in the field of sanitation is almost non-existent – limited to infrequent clean-ups of small areas led by churches or chiefs. So neither is there any cooperation among residents to deal with the problem directly; nor is there any

---

2 The attitude of some long-time residents (*nzika*) is also a factor, for they are sometimes seen to be rude to newcomers – breaking into queues ahead of them, for instance – as though they are of less consequence than themselves.

significant action – short of the imminent threat of a cholera outbreak – to compel the relevant authorities to overcome their inertia on the issue, as discussed in Chapter 4. In short, in Ndirande there is no equivalent of the potentially empowered citizenry or of the pent-up demand for better governance that figure in the usual donor and NGO discourse.

Ordinary people in Malawi are hardly more suited to the role of development 'principals' to which they are assigned in the current donor script than the politicians they support. Residents of Ndirande do not exercise 'voice' or 'demand accountability' from local government for several reasons. They include the facts that there is no easy point of access and that they have very low expectations of government as a provider of public goods. But more fundamentally, the population cannot come together and act as a collective.

This community of perhaps a half-million people is replete with social dilemmas or collective action problems, which are evidenced by an abundance of free-riders and tragedies of the commons. Each social dilemma on its own is complicated, but together they are more complex because they are nested, creating a set of multilevel and long-term non-developmental situations. Sometimes the problems are compounded by outsiders, such as aid agencies, who fail to understand their nature and advocate unhelpful solutions which get piled on top of other failing institutions. There are a few instances where citizens pull together to solve their own problems, but these institutions are generally not sustained and are narrowly focused because the environment in which they operate is not supportive of collective action. Where solutions are found, they often involve town chiefs (Cammack et al. 2009) and are to a greater or lesser extent hybrids of newer and older ways of doing things.

We illustrate these propositions with examples from the fields of sanitation and public health on the one hand, and public order and justice on the other. In collective action terms, these may be seen as a case of serious failure and two cases of qualified success.

The Nasolo river again We previously treated the abuse of the Nasolo river as the result of policy-driven institutional incoherence. However, from the point of view of Ndirande residents, the Nasolo is a common-pool resource that suffers from 'tragedy of the commons' – overuse, neglect and lack of management in the collective interest. Free-riding is widespread, as no one utilising the river takes responsibility for keeping it fit for use. This includes the chiefs whose jurisdictions it crosses, even though it is they (or their ancestors) who allocate(d) parcels of land in the villages along the river, and who continue to assert rights in the land – claiming a fee whenever plots change hands and hearing cases about parcels whose boundaries are along the river.

Few residents seem to care whether the river is unhealthy, or at least they do not care to the point of making a fuss about it or stopping free-riding on any efforts by others. One Health Surveillance Assistant typically attributed this to people's 'ignorance, carelessness and lack of *ubuntu*' – *ubuntu* being an expression common in southern Africa meaning 'our interconnectedness, our common humanity and the responsibility to each other that deeply flows from our deeply felt connection' (Nussbaum 2003: 2; Cammack 2012a: 20).

This being the case, the assumption that citizens – as principals – might care enough about the river to take action to compel chiefs, city officials, district environmental officers or local politicians to ensure its cleanliness is misconceived. We cannot assume therefore (as many donors and NGOs do) that strengthening civil society demand, by, for example, informing people about their rights, is a straightforward solution to the problem. In fact, if demand-side solutions are to be found, they have to start by discovering arrangements to deal with the problem of free-riding, not by ignoring its existence.

The Nasolo will remain a dangerous eyesore as long as no one takes responsibility for ensuring it is not mismanaged. In principle, common-pool resource dilemmas such as this can be addressed in a number of ways, but such actions require innovative thinking, strong incentives and new institutional frameworks. One way forward would call for the generation of usage rights and maintenance duties legitimized through local customs and individual interactions, as advocated by many specialists (e.g. Ostrom et al. 2002). This would involve defining rules that are locally rooted, understood and changeable by those who manage the river. However, in the circumstances we have described, it might be more practical to redesignate the river as a private resource whose use is reserved for those living on its banks or for a membership-only club.

Under this alternative, the members/residents would assume management and legal responsibility, monitor the behaviour of users and impose sanctions on those who offended. To make such a scheme effective would require coordination with higher layers of officialdom responsible for the environment. It would involve a recognition that in this instance, historical institutions (such as chiefs) as well as state agencies are ineffective protectors of the commons and need to be replaced – a radical idea.

Public order and security Our second example refers to the informal policing of Ndirande. Ndirande has two quite different parts – it has planned housing areas with streets laid out and paved, and it has squatter areas, where pathways between closely built houses are rocky, polluted and unkempt. In both sections there are Neighbourhood Watch (NW) groups consisting of guards who walk the streets and lanes at night, warning householders to keep their doors and windows locked and questioning any pedestrian who is out after the informal curfew.[3] Guards often carry sticks or pangas (machetes) and torches, which are supposed to be supplied by the community. In theory, NW guards are 'volunteers', but in fact they are generally paid a small wage. The money paid out for wages and equipment is raised by voluntary contributions from householders. Some residents say they have nothing worth stealing and so refuse to donate, while other poor people claim they do not have sufficient funds. Most NW groups are unstable in that their composition changes often. Sometimes they collapse altogether. In those cases, several months or more may pass before a new set of guards is recruited and sent out nightly. Despite this off-and-on existence, NW groups have been one factor contributing to falling crime rates in Ndirande.[4]

We interpret this in the following way. The relative success of the NW service is rooted in its adaption to local conditions. First, it answers a widely felt local need for security, one that became worse at the transition[5] and was met initially by brutal, local 'Inkatha' vigilantes. Secondly, it does so flexibly. While it was designed to be voluntary, it

---

3 Curfews are not established by law, but exist where chiefs, police and community elite have declared that they are required for security. They are generally set for 10 p.m., though bars in Ndirande were allowed to stay open till midnight. People driving cars are allowed to travel at night, so curfews target poorer (walking) populations.

4 Other contributions to falling rates are patrol cars that answer emergency calls and community policing committees which liaise with the police.

5 When the MCP's Young Pioneers – who performed police duties – were abolished at the same time that rule-bound institutions were weakened.

responded to the requirements of poor youth who need wages if they are to serve as guards. Thirdly, NW groups are overseen by chiefs – who historically have had their own guard forces to ensure village discipline.[6] This is the case in rural areas too, where most Ndirande residents originate. In other words, after moving into town migrants find institutions not unlike those which they have at home; they are operating within their 'cultural repertoire'. Finally, there is a practical integration with the formal structures of the state. NW groups interact with the community through local committees and with the police through a special liaison officer. NW guards are trained and equipped to some level by the police, and have official recognition to the extent that they can detain suspects and haul them off to a police station. They are sometimes called upon to give testimony in court.

Thus, NW as it has evolved is a practical, locally rooted hybrid institution that meets a perceived need in a way that is both legal and culturally appropriate. The NW system works as well as it does because some collective action problems have been addressed. The residents contribute (more or less voluntarily) to a fund overseen by the chief. Their willingness to do so is affected by the fact that they know well whether or not security is being provided because they are stopped by the NW if out after curfew and hear of arrests of thieves and other criminals. Finally, the force is seen as historically legitimate because Malawians are familiar with chiefs' enforcers. It is also rooted in the law (though some of the actions of guards may not be).[7]

A similar experience based on a Neighbourhood Watch idea derived from UK experience has been documented in APPP-supported research in Tanzania. There too, efforts that were not tailored to the local context ended in failure but subsequent adjustments succeeded, for broadly the reasons observed in Malawi (Cross 2011).

Bwalo justice as a public good This is our third illustration and our second case of qualified success (Cammack 2012a: 31–2). Malawi has a formal judiciary ranging from the supreme court and the high court down to various grades of magistrate's court. In 2011 a law was passed

---

6 Further, some chiefs still have their own 'boys' who enforce their orders.

7 NW guards are known to beat up pedestrians who don't immediately obey them. Further, the informal pedestrian curfews established by chiefs and enforced by guards are probably not constitutional.

to create a local court system, but this idea has not been popular – for fear these local courts would be too much like Kamuzu Banda's rights-abusive 'traditional courts'. The nearest court to Ndirande is the magistrate's court at Machinjiri, which handles cases of petty theft and disturbing the peace[8] among others. In Blantyre is the high court, which handles major criminal and civil cases.

For everyday disputes many residents in Ndirande turn to the various chiefs' *bwalo* courts for adjudication. The reasons appear to be because, first, they are inexpensive – sometimes costing a *chibwalo* fee of K500 (about $3.30 in 2010) to access them. Secondly, they are close – held in the same village, usually on the ground in front of the chief's house. Further, bwalo courts are found in virtually every village in Malawi, run by village headmen, so people know them as legitimate institutions. And while the laws being enforced differ from place to place (and from chief to chief), they are similar enough to be recognisable to Ndirande residents originating from anywhere in the country. According to chiefs, the laws they apply are based on 'common sense' or 'local custom', which also makes sense to residents.[9] That the chiefs have specialist knowledge – e.g. the ability to recognise witches when ordinary people cannot – is apparently accepted as well.

The language of the court is the local language (Chichewa in Ndirande) and ordinary people do not find the courts' procedures difficult to understand. The courts are public – sometimes with spectators in the galleries who are recognised by the arbiter and able to offer comment. The defendant, if dissatisfied with the head-man's judgment, can appeal upwards to the group village headman and beyond that, to the Traditional Authority (senior chief), both of whom will have a bwalo court. They are also free to take their complaints to the formal court system. Finally, unlike the more formal courts, bwalo courts seek to reconcile community members rather than punish offenders.

Bwalo courts handle a wide variety of cases, all of which reflect

---

8 This can include persons thought to be witches but the Witchcraft Act (1911), which implies that witchcraft is not real, makes it hard to deal with such cases, so the law against behaviour likely to cause public disorder is used.

9 It seems natural that a person from one ethnic group (e.g. a northern Tonga) abides by rules in a distant community where another ethnicity dominates (as do the Lomwe in Ndirande).

the ordinary problems residents face on a daily basis and the types of issues that divide them. The judgments appear to reflect the views of the community generally, for people appear to obey judgments and observers' views, often exclaimed aloud during a trial, are considered.

For instance, a man accused of witchcraft by his neighbours and family will be given the opportunity to apologise, renounce the practice, and resettle in the community. He will remain there safely unless he begins practising witchcraft again.[10] Those who are obstinate and refuse to admit to being witches will not be dealt with as kindly by the community or the court; some will have their houses destroyed and/or be sent out of the village by the chief.[11] Similarly, people who belong to a savings club[12] and fail to contribute their fair share to its members will be forced to pay up by the chief, who will oversee the collection and dispersal of monies due. A man who impregnates a girl and refuses to care for her and the child will be told he must contribute to their livelihoods. Land illicitly claimed as part of an inheritance will be returned to its rightful owner. Petty thieves will be ordered to pay restitution, and those causing accidental loss will be expected to reimburse and apologise to the owner. Fighting women will be chastised and told to make up and behave. In many such cases the chief or *nduna* (chief's adviser) will conclude with homilies that reinforce community values.

In Ndirande, where people live cheek by jowl and under the grinding weight of poverty, the service provided by bwalo courts is of great importance. One may have reservations about particular judgments or about the bodies of law or shared beliefs that are being applied – for example, on witchcraft. However, the results need to be compared with what would be the most likely result of such disputes in their absence. The lack of alternatives in the form of cheap, comprehensible and accessible formal courts also enhances the value of bwalo justice. That they are linked informally to the state judicial system – through referrals and references to cases in the magistrate's and high courts – adds to their usefulness. Their limitation – like any other action

---

10 An illness, accident or death in the community can demonstrate he has reverted to his old ways.

11 The formal law and courts, on the other hand, will only prosecute someone who admits to 'pretending to be a witch'.

12 These consist of small groups whose members donate the same amount of money in a period, and each of them in rotation receives the whole amount.

by chiefs[13] – is that people can ignore them and their judgments. Yet the fact that bwalo courts meet regularly in busy villages and are packed by litigants and observers indicates their importance to communities at large.

West African stories about practical hybridity

As well as investigating the local governance of public goods provision in the four areas of maternal health, water and sanitation, market management and security, APPP researchers looked at two sectoral reform initiatives that seemed likely to shed light on the meaning of 'working with the grain'. One was local justice provision in Ghana – a very different country setting from that of Malawi – and the other focused on public education reforms in three francophone countries of West Africa. Both studies shed additional light on the meaning and usefulness of practical hybrid institutions.

Practical hybridity in local justice and dispute resolution The provision of accessible justice and dispute resolution is recognised as a fundamental duty of the state in Africa, as elsewhere. However, throughout the region the institutions of state justice are struggling with problems of overload, perceived corruption and public distrust. Current policy prescriptions for improving access and trust are dominated by the belief that these will be better provided by non-state arrangements, including customary (chiefs') courts and informal arrangements of Alternative Dispute Resolution (ADR). APPP research in Ghana has challenged this point of view, drawing on a large-scale multi-method comparative study of three types of current provision (Crook et al. 2010; Crook 2011; Crook 2012).

As we have seen, in Malawi chiefs' courts fill what would otherwise be a huge gap in what seems a practical way. The Ghana context is different, however. The range of institutions is more diverse and provides more judicial solutions. Chiefs and chiefs' courts occupy a different place among the options for local people seeking to resolve their disputes.

---

13 Chiefs are legally recognised, have defined jurisdictions and duties, and if hereditary they are generally paid a stipend by the state. But they come under the Ministry of Local Government and senior chiefs are appointed by the president, so their powers are limited by politicians, including MPs, and technocrats (Cammack et al. 2009).

The conclusion from the Ghana study is that ADR-type accessible justice is available at local level in Ghana. It owes its legitimacy, accessibility and effectiveness to its alignment with popular beliefs and expectations. However, the vehicles that deliver this service most reliably are not the neo-traditional Customary Land Secretariat courts but the mediation services attached to the first-instance magistrate's courts and, in particular, those provided by the Commission on Human Rights and Administrative Justice (CHRAJ), a constitutional body established in 1992.

An initial survey provided some empirical insight into citizens' opinions about what makes a dispute settlement fair and morally acceptable. Both the magistrate's courts and the CHRAJ were rated as highly congruent with these beliefs. CHRAJ mediations, which are run by full-time, specially trained professionals, scored very highly for accessibility. The magistrates also did relatively well by conducting procedures informally, using local languages and drawing on a variety of legal codes, including customary law and cultural principles such as respect for the elderly. The customary land courts, in contrast, were very formal in their procedures and seen as intimidating to women and immigrants. On effectiveness, as measured by litigant satisfaction, CHRAJ procedures were rated as best, and the chiefs' courts as worst, for speed and cost, while the enforceability of the remedies of the overloaded magistrate's courts was seen as a countervailing strength.

All three types of local justice service covered in the Ghana research could be considered hybrid institutions. However, what emerges strongly from the findings is that the form of hybridity matters, as well as the country context. The arrangements that are rated highest for legitimacy, accessibility and effectiveness are those that combine congruence with local values and expectations with the motivation and skill-sets provided by a specialised state agency. This practical hybridity seems a more likely formula for success, applicable in many other countries that share Ghana's English common-law tradition, than either civil or neo-traditional mechanisms disconnected from the state.

Practical hybridity in the design of public education Similar conclusions were reached independently in research on religion and educational reform experiments (Villalón and Tidjani-Alou 2012). The research explored the sources and implications of reforms to the public education systems of three countries of the West African Sahel region, Mali, Niger and Senegal (Villalón and Bodian 2012; Villalón et al. 2012). These reforms attempt to address the unpopularity and poor educational performance of the government school systems by incorporating elements that reflect Muslim values and expectations while also ensuring training of pupils for future employment. The findings suggest that incorporating religion into programmes has been highly effective in encouraging parents to send children, especially girls, to public schools. The main risk is that of overburdening students and stretching curricula too thinly.

The researchers conclude that, in the Sahelian educational context, building institutions that work with or tap into prevailing moral orders and cultural values shows real promise as a means to address some deeply entrenched obstacles to better educational and, therefore, development outcomes. This is consistent with Kelsall's (2008b) proposition that development efforts have a greater chance of success when they stop treating cultural factors as a problem and try instead to harness them as a means to channel behaviour in more positive ways.

Strikingly, however, while the cases suggest the importance of local institutions, they do not suggest a rejection of the state as a primary actor in development. Significant popular demand for education in the Sahel takes the state model as its point of departure, but asks that it be adjusted to local concerns. Again, therefore, the 'grain' of popular demand in contemporary Africa is not a desire for 'traditional' institutions, but rather for modern state structures that have been adapted to, or infused with, contemporary cultural preferences.

Other research carried out with APPP support in the DRC suggests interesting parallels (Leinweber 2012a, 2012b). Provision of education by Christian churches in a nominal partnership with the Congolese state is long established and its recent contribution to a form of negotiated state-building has been well documented (Titeca and De Herdt 2011). Less familiar is the process whereby the Muslim minority under a reformist leadership has overcome its former fragmentation and quiescence in order to participate more fully in the liberalised political system. In this context, it has been organising its own schools. Like the Catholic schools, these are part of the formal structure of public education, regulated in principle by the government, but benefiting from the support of a faith-based community.

Associational life and local problem-solving in Niger

We have expressed the view that donor and NGO initiatives often go wrong because they promote solutions that do not address the real constraints under which people live and interact with each other. They do better when they recognise the prevalence of multilevel collective action problems than when they try to force local realities into a principal–agent mould, as in 'demand for good governance' types of intervention. APPP research did not make a systematic study of aid-funded interventions, as its interest was in the broader question of institutions that work for development. Nevertheless, we came across enough examples of aid-driven failure, both in the fieldwork and in our searches of related research literature, to justify some conclusions on the subject. The Niger fieldwork was a particularly rich source of insight, not only on how aid does harm but also on how it might easily become more supportive of sub-national problem-solving efforts or 'local reforms'.

In Niger, the general pattern is that the various 'committees' and other associational structures promoted by donors tend to 'end up being dissolved or falling asleep' (Olivier de Sardan et al. 2010a: 15). With the single exception of the transport stations mentioned in Chapter 4, sanitation and cleansing matters are seriously neglected, and the collective cleaning of public places that used to occur under the more authoritarian regimes of the past is now rare, a common view being that this is now the responsibility of local government. The neighbourhood committees for the management of household waste that were established by the municipal authorities in two of the three Niger study sites provide a rich illustration of the problems with what we might call the 'associational' approach to public provision (Issa 2011: 39–42). The Niger field reports speak in similar terms about the collapse of the market management committees established by the municipalities in two sites. The point is made that, even though these were all initiatives of the mayors' offices (with, in the case of household waste, support from the Dutch NGO SNV), the 'institutional engineering' was of the aid-funded project type, the municipalities having tended to adopt this organisational model and make it their own (Olivier de Sardan et al. 2010a: 18; Oumarou 2011: 27–40).

As Olivier de Sardan summarises: 'Neighbourhood sanitation committees, borehole management committees for drinking water, market management committees, all present in all three municipalities, are good examples. End of the support, end of the committees! There may be exceptions to this maxim of course, but it was confirmed in our study sites' (2012b: 4).

Money and motivation One factor that may be suspected of underlying this pattern – which is by no means restricted to Niger – is the widespread availability of supplementary donor funding for performance enhancement, training workshops and meetings of all kinds. In many countries, this has had a corrosive effect on the willingness of countless individuals at all levels from the Permanent Secretary to the street cleaner to perform public duties without special inducement. Within the civil service or public administration, the fact that enhanced remuneration and conditions are associated with the project modality of funding has created a 'two-speed administration' (Blundo 2011b). However, the problem is a more general one, with the 'hunt for per diems' coming to characterise the public service in general in many countries (Soreide et al. 2012). At local levels, too, the reserves of volunteerism and dutiful community service that used to exist have given way to an almost universal hunger for ways to access different forms of 'development rent' (Olivier de Sardan 2012b: 13–19).

The damage done by this to the potential for local collective action is considerable, as suggested by the path-breaking book on Pakistan by Bano (2012). Bano starts from the empirical generalisation that, in Pakistan and elsewhere, civic groups that get funding from development agencies end up with no members. She then explains why this happens, drawing on collective action analysis in the Ostrom tradition. The leaders of successful self-help organisations are normally motivated not by pure altruism, as donors tend to assume, but by psycho-social rewards, such as honour, prestige and fame. Members of such organisations know this and can monitor behaviour that signals that sort of motivation. This, in turn, enables them to overcome the mistrust that would otherwise weaken their willingness to join collective actions. When aid funds are seen to be received by leaders, however, this undermines this simple mechanism by which members are assured of their leaders' trustworthiness. The end result is that new members do not join and the original members tend to leave.

This powerful explanation reinforces the importance of viewing development through the lens of collective action problems and solutions. It may, on its own, account for a good deal of what follows in this section. However, the political economy of trying to use aid to foster self-help is complicated in other ways too. Donor money, whether channelled through official projects or NGOs, comes with strings attached. These include organisational templates that serve donor accountability purposes, not the aim of facilitating local problem-solving. Such impositions may well do actual harm to existing or potential instruments of self-help.

Aid-driven associational models The approach we propose to call 'associational' has been promoted strongly by official aid donors, who see it as the natural counterpart of building or rebuilding the legal-rational foundations of the state. It is central to the concepts of 'civil society strengthening' and building 'demand for good governance' that have informed governance interventions since the mid-2000s. It has been part of the core ideology of most Northern NGOs for even longer. These days, it is also very much part of the thinking and work practices of national and local governments and NGOs and has been thoroughly 'appropriated' by them, although in a more or less distorted form (Olivier de Sardan 2009b: 16). Its centrepiece is the organisational model of the 'voluntary association'.

Voluntary associations have members (and thus non-members), formalised rules (and thus formal sanctions), governance arrangements (and thus scope for the use and abuse of power) and funding needs (and thus a host of accounting and reporting requirements). Even when they take the form of 'community-based organisations', when, in principle, the membership includes the whole local population, these characteristics remain.

The main thrust of a large case-study literature is that initiatives based on the associational model tend not to work, or not in the way their promoters intend. They create new forms of inequality, increase materialistic motivations and quite often promote corruption and clientelism among leaders. They are divisive from a social point of view, privileging those who have the education and other skills needed to comply with the funder's requirements. They tend to get diverted from addressing people's real problems (pulled instead into the donor business of 'finding problems for solutions'), and often end up weakening the members' capacity for collective action, rather than strengthening it.

What Olivier de Sardan (ibid.: 14–18) calls the 'associational mode of local governance' requires the recipients of financial assistance to organise themselves according to definite norms imported from the outside and laid down in some detail by the funding body. Norms that are supposed to ensure accountable management of aid permit social advancement by those able to master donor ways of thinking, while demobilising communities and creating new sources of social exclusion. The literature on this point is substantial and growing.

For example, Swidler and Watkins' (2009) account of NGO-promoted self-help on HIV and AIDS in Malawi is very persuasive on the social downsides of the standard approach. Emphasising the way donor-funded projects become a source of social differentiation and exclusion, it echoes the arguments of Uvin (1998) about the negative social impacts of aid in pre-genocide Rwanda. Gugerty and Kremer (2008) studied external funding for women's community groups in Kenya using a quantitative impact assessment technique. The strongest effect they found was on group membership and leadership, these being skewed towards younger, better-educated and better-off women. In this way, the groups gradually lost the characteristics that drew the funders to them in the first place.

Igoe (2003) has given us a detailed account of the effects of donor support to pastoralist land rights movements in East Africa, which involved turning them into NGOs. The energies of leaders were diverted into activities that could be justified in aid funding reports at the expense of the objectives and solidarities with which the movement started out. Several of the same themes recur in Dill's (2009, 2010) accounts of the lack of 'fit' between NGO-promoted community-based organisations and the local sociocultural environment in Dar es Salaam and Blundo's (2009) study of NGO sanitation initiatives in a Niger town. Also relevant are Lange's (2008) and Manor's (2007: 21) findings on the destructive institutional side effects of single-sector user committees or stakeholder committees, and Vajja and White's (2008) conclusions about World Bank Social Funds in Malawi and Zambia as users, not generators, of social capital.

Enabling local reforms

APPP fieldwork not only provided negative examples of the kind outlined above. It has also given us a handle on various departures from the standard associational model of self-help that seem to work rather better. Alternative models are not easy to find but do exist, albeit in imperfect forms, even in very poor countries like Malawi and Niger. What they have in common is that they are locally anchored in that they address the collective action problems that the relevant stakeholders actually face in specific local or sectoral conditions. They do not involve generic models of best practice derived from decontextualised global experience.

Our Malawi research gives some pointers to what locally anchored problem-solving looks like on the ground. Some of these involve the phenomenon of 'town chiefs', the local leaders who are present in many urban neighbourhoods and play a significant role, partly on account of the non-implementation since 2005 of the Local Government Act and the resulting absence of formal local councils. We have already met town chiefs in the context of the weakness of local action on sanitation and the relative success of the Neighbourhood Watch initiative and bwalo courts in Ndirande. Here we provide a few more details.

Some town chiefs have historic roots in that they claim heredi-tary titles corresponding to rural areas that have been engulfed by the expanding city. Others have emerged spontaneously in the last fifteen years in the context of accelerated urbanisation. Others were appointed as block leaders under the decentralisation reforms of the 1990s and have stayed on. The expression 'town chiefs' covers a number of different sorts of leadership role, showing affinities with 'royal' chieftaincy in some places and with party-political authority in others. Residents call all these types of leader *mfumu*, or chief. Although origins vary, there seem to be commonalities, including some ability to mobilise collective action by residents of different backgrounds and to claim a legitimacy that is not rooted in any specific ethnicity but in principles and cultural repertoires that are held to be common to the traditions of several of the Malawian 'tribes' (Cammack et al. 2009). For all its inadequacies, the town chiefs phenomenon suggests what can happen when, for some reason, no 'universal' organisational model is implemented forcefully by the government, their donor advisers or NGOs.

The smaller urban areas covered in the Malawi study also give us some examples of critical public goods issues apparently being addressed by local cooperative effort in ways that are not observed in Ndirande. The instances of promising collective problem-solving that have been observed all seem to be associated with acts of initiative and imagination by local leaders who occupy official positions, a District Chief Executive Officer in one case and an officially recognised paramount chief in the other (Cammack and Kanyongolo 2010: 29–30). As in the Niger experiences discussed below, not just legitimacy but unusual leadership qualities, even charisma, seem to be an element in all of the more promising ventures. NGO or aid funding is not necessarily absent in these cases. In fact, some of the promising experiences do involve NGOs as actors, and some involve the use of project funds. However, in no cases are they primarily NGO or project initiatives, or driven by the supply of ideas and money from the outside. They are hybrids.

The Niger researchers use the term 'local reforms' or 'reforms from the inside' (Olivier de Sardan 2009a: 116–18) to identify a particularly interesting type of initiative. They distinguish such initiatives from merely palliative adjustments to the inadequacy of state provision.

The latter are much more common and include a great variety of gap-filling solutions. They include acts of ad hoc public duty, as when a mayor's office advances the fuel that a family needs for transporting a pregnant woman to an emergency centre. They also extend to acts of charity or *noblesse oblige*, for example when a sub-chief pays the ambulance driver from his own pocket, or where a local dignitary repairs a broken-down vehicle at personal expense. More often, perhaps, they involve some form of informal privatisation of the service by the provider, involving illegal user charges or corruption.

It may be argued that even when they are barely legitimate, adjustments of this kind have a positive side, in that they permit a service to be provided that would not otherwise be provided (Olivier de Sardan 2012b: 3–5). In the Sahelian forest services, for example, the collection of 'fines' is largely but not entirely predatory. It sometimes funds a common fund or 'kitty' that serves, at least in part, to address the local forestry team's otherwise severe shortages of transport and other equipment (Blundo forthcoming: 13). However, we think it would be wrong to qualify this as a successful local reform.

A better example of a local reform in Niger is the initiative discussed more than once in the previous chapters under which a number of districts began collecting 'a few additional pennies' from all users of primary health-care facilities to fund the fuel and staff costs associated with emergency evacuations of pregnant women. This was a bottom-up initiative, but rather unusually it was not informal. It was validated by the health teams of the district and their Management Committees, though without consulting the ministry and without the ministry's agreement or support. It was a form of user charge but the costs were spread over time and over the whole population of health-centre users, providing a mechanism akin to a health insurance scheme. As we have explained, the Ministry of Health took the view that this form of user contribution was contrary to the official policy of exemption from health charges, and forbade health centres from taking the 100 CFA francs from the parents of under-fives. At one blow, the flow of funds dried up, and the situation returned to what prevailed before.

One of the things that distinguishes this case of 'local reform' from reform initiatives in general is that it was initiated locally and aimed to solve a specific problem to which national policies and leaders were not offering solutions. It also relied primarily on mobilising local resources, and, above all, was *not* driven by the availability of donor funds, directly or through government. For this reason, no organisational templates had to be adopted, and it was possible to draw on local views about what was important, proper and acceptable in addressing the problem. It was also a 'bridging' reform that revealed a capability for self-help based on nation-wide networking.

This might suggest that development assistance should have no role at all in local reforms. However, that would be a premature conclusion. A somewhat unexpected aspect of the additional pennies story concerns the role apparently played by aid personnel in getting the initiative started. The details remain unclear, but it seems that the solution was first suggested by locally embedded staff of Belgian Technical Cooperation (BTC). Crucially, that agency did not intervene directly and did not provide any financial support, with all of the perverse consequences that this would most likely have entailed. The input was just an idea. Commenting on this aspect, the Niger researchers concluded: 'Engaging with local informal initiatives and helping them to become institutionalised would be a better strategy than ignoring them ... [D]iscreet and responsive support to local reformers and to institutionalisation "from the bottom up" should become more central to the official strategies of development agencies' (Olivier de Sardan 2012a).

We agree, and think this is relevant more generally. The development business needs to become much more focused on enabling initiatives that are 'locally anchored', where this means being driven by local problem-solving – whether at the community level or within the multi-stakeholder environments that are a feature of so much public goods provision in Africa today. We have suggested that direct funding of groups and organisations means, inevitably, specifying institutional templates, for control and accountability purposes if nothing else. This can have very negative effects on capacities for genuine self-help, even if the money itself does not do the sort of harm emphasised by Bano. Therefore, more attention should be given to the enabling environment for initiatives that are both technically sensible and locally anchored, if necessary drawing heavily on locally established ways of doing things.

Summing up

The research reported in this chapter confirms that, in spite of everything, local problem-solving does exist. The factors that constrain or undermine it include donor money and donor associational templates. A mass of new funding can change the nature of local initiatives by changing incentives and skewing behaviour. Generic templates fail because good institutions solve the collective action problems as they are posed in particular contexts. As a rule, arrangements that work well borrow institutional understandings from local society – they are practical hybrids, marrying up modern professional standards or scientific principles with established practices in the area.

The implications of these findings are far-reaching for reformers in Africa and for international development agencies alike. Much of the evidence we have considered may seem simply 'anti-aid'. However, it is more complicated than that. Aid can and does do harm, but particularly when it takes the form of a transfer of funds and ideas based on the false premise that the constraints being faced are some sort of principal–agent problem. With few exceptions, they are more likely to be problems of collective action.

That may mean that people should be left alone to find their own solutions. But, at the very least, external actors have a duty to contribute to the creation of an enabling environment for local problem-solving, for example by not supporting the sort of policy rigidity that killed off the extra pennies scheme in Niger. In addition, because collective action problems are, by definition, not easily soluble by those directly involved, there may be some scope for a third party to facilitate useful change. This, perhaps, was the contribution offered by the BTC personnel in Niger.

But this is a challenging kind of work for development and technical assistance agencies and even NGOs as presently constituted. It requires the nature of the problem to be well understood. It requires the intervening agent to have the flexibility, learning capacity and intellectual modesty to play a facilitation role successfully. Several of these qualities are in short supply in the development business as it stands, partly because of the way aid is currently led and financed in the North. But this is not entirely inevitable, as we argue in the Conclusion.

CONCLUSION

Countries of low-income Africa are once again experiencing sustained economic growth, and several indicators of human well-being are steadily improving too. But African development is not yet on a safe upward path. Current growth is not bringing widespread productivity gains or leading to structural economic change. Smallholder agriculture, on which the majority in most countries still depends, remains untransformed, and partly as a consequence, new sources of gainful employment are not being generated. The social indicators that are improving are mainly in the bio-medical field, where international efforts behind a good technical fix – a new vaccine, better mosquito nets – have paid dividends. When it comes to routine public services and regulation in the areas where ordinary people live, conditions remain abysmal in most places. Even the bio-medical fixes are hindered by institutional problems manifested in corruption, inefficiency or waste, to the point where, in notorious instances, international funders have been obliged to suspend their aid.

This is not inevitable. A succession of countries in Asia that within living memory were as poor as most of the countries of sub-Saharan Africa have radically transformed their economies, starting with smallholder agriculture. They have turned their public agencies into efficient providers of services and regulatory public goods to large populations. It *can* be done. But at the moment in most of Africa, it is not happening. Understanding exactly why is a vital challenge, for the people of Africa and for the future of the world.

Governance for development: turning the ship around

As we argued at the beginning of this book, the answers that have usually been given to questions of this sort over the last quarter of a century are seriously misleading. Furthermore, these wrong answers have been massively influential, not least within Africa itself. Worldwide, generations of young idealists have grown up with the belief that solutions to African poverty are simple. In Europe, the dominant view has been that 'making poverty history' is largely a matter of funding massive resource transfers. In Africa, there are few people who place that sort of trust in international aid, and many who harbour suspicions about the motives behind it. However, another set of global ideas is widely accepted, often with even less critical examination. To develop, Africa needs 'good governance': African elites are typically too greedy and selfish; the African masses suffer the consequences but are unaware of their rights; therefore, progressively minded people should be building a civil society that enables ordinary citizens to claim their rights and demand accountability of their leaders.

We have given reasons for thinking that each step in this line of argument is flawed. Most fundamentally, the identification of developmental governance with 'good governance', where this is defined in terms that reflect the most recent phase in the institutional development of the democratic capitalist North, is seriously mistaken. Even a cursory glance at the facts of history shows what is wrong with it. Liberal-democratic free-market capitalism has never been a feasible option for a poor country wanting to become a richer country, and it is not a precondition for the economic and social transformations that poor countries need. If it were, neither Germany nor South Korea, and neither Sweden nor Malaysia, would be where they are today. To the extent that these countries are now democratic, it is because they have each developed economically first.

'Good governance' is an ideological construct, not a scientific concept or one whose association with desirable development outcomes is supported by evidence. While democracy is a worthwhile goal in Africa, there are few of the institutions that are required for it to flourish. These depend on the creation of a middle class, with education, productive wealth and networks that create bonds across social divisions nationwide. Northern development agencies have not read their history and have tried to extend the benefits of their systems of government to African states prematurely. African activists, for their part, tend to draw conclusions too directly from their experience of well-functioning institutions in the countries where they have studied. In reality, however, democratic electioneering, decentralisation and many of the other attributes of fully fledged Northern democracy combine badly with neopatrimonial institutions. In the African context, they generate vacillating economic policies, elite capture of rents that could be used to provide public goods and party systems that provide no alternative programme or vision. This has been apparent for some time. Yet the ideological movement around good governance has squeezed out most thoughts about progressive and yet locally rooted options for Africa. For the last twenty-five years – roughly since the end of the Cold War – this poorly considered agenda has prevented rational, evidence-based thinking on governance for development.

We are not the first to say this. In fact, in regard to this first flaw in the typical argument about African governance, there could be said to be an expert consensus. At the World Bank, for example, rejection of one-size-fits-all governance remedies, and the will to replace 'best practice' with 'good fit' approaches to institutional design, is at least a decade old. For almost as long – as shown by our brief scan of the literature in Chapter 1 – economists and political scientists have been condemning policy advice that 'kicks away the ladder' by which the now-rich countries climbed to their current position of wealth and power (Chang 2002). There is wide acceptance, in principle, of Grindle's (2004) appeal for institutional reforms that are appropriate to context and 'good enough' to meet the most urgent developmental challenges of the moment.

Yet, as we went on to argue in Chapter 1, this expert consensus has not driven a turnaround in practice, among either aid donors or African reformers. The reasons, of course, include the fact that the experts do not hold the purse strings in the aid business, and those who do are often too preoccupied with spending their budgets to be attracted by novel programming approaches. The reform activists, for their part, are generally small players in the domestic politics of their countries. So mere intellectual conversion among the more thoughtful development practitioners and their academic advisers cannot be expected to make much of a dent in the dominant players' perspectives. But there is also another reason, we have suggested. This is that advocates of the new expert consensus (and we do not exclude ourselves from this criticism) have been insufficiently clear about the implications of their position.

In many respects, the new thinking about governance that prevails in the most advanced parts of the development business (in, say, the best corners of the World Bank or DfID) still looks a lot like the old thinking. The general idea of seeking 'good fit' governance and of recognising that very different sorts of institution can perform key functions in development is acknowledged in principle. Staff are even trained to study country contexts using the best tools of applied political economy analysis. But actual programming is rarely changed as a result. Rather than starting from a locally informed and realistic take on what needs to be done to get improvements, new governance interventions reproduce the essential features of previous programmes.

Thus, the second, third and fourth steps in the typical line of argument alluded to above continue to be taken: African elites are basically (and peculiarly) immoral; the ordinary citizens of African countries do share the goals of development agencies, but they lack information and awareness; therefore, a good use of aid resources is to empower the citizenry by making them aware of their 'rights' and how to demand more accountable, more development-oriented, leadership. Score cards for community monitoring of services, civil-society strengthening and other social accountability schemes of the kinds that have been rolled out continuously for the last fifteen years or so are the result. With no real challenge to the mainstream good governance consensus, the ship has not even begun to turn around.

Old thinking masquerading as new thinking

How this has happened and what it would take to really turn things around has been the subject of this book. Our contention is that what needs to happen is for governance challenges to be seen less in terms of principal–agent problems and more as unresolved collective action problems.

A decade ago, senior advisers at the World Bank recognised publicly in a way they had not done before the problem of non-developmental political leadership on the African continent. The principal–agent perspective, which had guided public sector reforms up to that point, remained valid, but was too managerialist and apolitical; it was no longer realistic to see presidents and cabinets as the good guys, and as merely needing help to get lazy or demotivated civil servants and other public providers to do their jobs properly. The problem was deeper, they argued, and it did not originate with the public servants (World Bank 2003; Levy 2004). In our view, the logical next step would have been to probe further the sources of elite political preferences, getting to grips with the basic drivers of power politics in different sorts of developing country. While some research like this was begun, the trend-setters at the World Bank went a different way. Instead of opening up the black box of political incentives, they shifted the focus to a different set of 'principals' (citizens and service users) with the argument that development agencies might reasonably redirect some of their efforts to empowering these groups to monitor and regulate the activities of their 'agents' – political leaders, officials and service providers. More recently the topic of elite politics and development has come to be addressed in a different way, with several teams of researchers picking up the insights of Mushtaq Khan (1995, 2010) and North, Wallis and Weingast (2009).

Those now contributing to this work include some of those who led the earlier change of view at the World Bank (see especially North et al. 2013). However, in the early 2000s such a move seems to have been considered either inconceivable or impractical, at least in and around the Bank. Instead, the most radical advocates of a more 'political' approach simply turned the previous principal–agent framework on its head.

This turn at the top of the aid business gave a new lease of life to all versions of the principal–agent perspective based on the idea of stimulating 'demand' for better governance, including the democratic decentralisation movement. It generated a new wave of interest in 'client power' and community monitoring of public services. Assisted latterly by the advance of accessible information technologies, it also led to an explosion of interest in 'social accountability', where civil-society advocacy meets community monitoring. As we saw at the end of Chapter 1, the popularity of these 'magic bullets' was more to do with the general appeal of working on the demand side of governance, given the then dominant ideological currents in the aid world, than the result of an accumulation of new evidence on the subject. Social science theory grounded empirically in developing-country contexts pointed, then as now, to different problems and different solutions.

Turning the principal–agent perspective on its head is not good enough. The reality revealed by research and African experience is that *neither* political leaders *nor* ordinary citizens can be counted on, in most places most of the time, as development principals. In due course, this may change, with new interests emerging that give priority to development goals and public goods. The reason that this is not yet happening is not that either group is morally deficient or slow witted. Instead, both face collective action problems when it comes to acting in their wider and longer-term best interests and in objectively developmental ways. Besides, as we suggested in Chapter

4, people and leaders together have found ways of meeting their immediate needs for goods and services that are more reliable and effective than waiting for the state to provide them.

What researchers at the Gothenburg QoG Institute have been arguing about why standard anti-corruption interventions do not work (Persson et al. 2010; Rothstein 2011) applies more generally to why so much else fails in the development business. The precise content and dimensions of the collective action problems that inhibit development efforts in any given context are the most relevant question for researchers. They ought also to be the central concern of African political leaders, governance activists and development donors.

What matters and why

So far, we have limited ourselves to restating and slightly elaborating what we set out in the Introduction and Chapter 1. In the following chapters, we took several further steps, which we now review. Starting with what shapes basic public goods delivery, we established that the immediate factors that affect performance in one key area – services and regulation for maternal health – are not those that have been emphasised by governments and the development business under the influence of the recent fashions in democratic decentralisation, client power and social accountability. In fact, the key drivers have very little at all to do with the 'demand side' of governance. To recapitulate, the three factors that emerged from the evidence as making a difference were:

- whether or not the de facto policy regime, including organisational mandates and resource flows, in the sector is internally coherent;
- the extent to which the national political leadership motivates and disciplines the multiple actors responsible for the quality of provision; and
- the degree to which there is an enabling environment that promotes or at least permits problem-solving at sub-national levels of the delivery system.

As we went on to argue in Chapters 4 and 5, these same three variables also explain much of the observed variation in delivery and delivery blockages in the areas of water and sanitation, market management and public order and security.

Such findings are hardly unprecedented. That these should be critical variables influencing the willingness and ability of providers to overcome key bottlenecks in provision could almost be described as common sense. On the other hand, it is not a fashionable view or one that can count on easy acceptance. These are issues that are rarely tackled by development programmers. Our findings run against the current of global policy thinking and hark back in several respects to older concerns in development administration that have passed out of favour. They passed out of favour partly because they were formulated in purely administrative terms, and the remedies then adopted were managerialist. In contrast, we have added an explicitly political dimension.

The coherence of policy, for example, is a very traditional concern in public administration. But in this book we have argued that it is time to recognise the reasons why policy and institutional frameworks are persistently and perhaps increasingly incoherent in many sectors. The biggest problems in this area are caused by donors and governments laying down new policies without bringing previous policies to a conclusion, and by populist appeals (intensified by the advent of multiparty elections) by presidents and presidential candidates, who instigate changes without regard for their implementation. These are the root problems that need to be addressed.

The second factor, discipline and motivation in public services, was, of course, the classic concern of the second-generation liberalisation reforms which succeeded first-generation structural-adjustment prescriptions for African countries in the 1990s. We have made explicit that the source of ill-discipline is the way countries are led politically, and not the way civil servants choose to behave. But we have also gone farther than most of the already large band of doubters about the effectiveness of traditional civil service reforms. Rather than declaring the roots of the problem to be political but leaving the politics inside a black box, we have sought to open it up.

Lining up in this respect with Kelsall (2013) and North et al. (2013), we have pinpointed the crucial significance of the way in which elites in different countries and at different stages of development establish a practical power equilibrium, or political settlement, with a tacit understanding about how to share major economic rents. The crucial question, therefore, is how and why political regimes differ across a spectrum of neopatrimonial types.

In a brief exploration of the 'why' question with particular reference to the forces that drive development in Rwanda, we suggested that such differences are not preordained: they are the result of more or less conscious choices by members of the national elite. However, like most other choices in development, these decisions involve problems of collective action. By definition, problems of collective action are not easily overcome. History suggests, and the case of Rwanda confirms, that elites overcome the collective action problems that ordinarily keep them focused on the short term when, and perhaps only when, they experience a sharp shock and or a sustained threat to their existence. The role of a strong leader with a compelling vision should not be discounted in these contexts, but the fundamental question is what it takes to construct a political settlement that favours economic and social transformation. That is about solving typical collective action logjams among the different components of the national elite.

Finally, the idea that successful development administration has problem-solving at its centre is not new either. It was compellingly argued, in the context of development projects, in the 1980s and after.[1] The interest in 'adaptive' approaches has been usefully revived recently by Andrews et al. (2012), but so far it has not been connected to two themes which we feel are important.

One is the way in which line ministries, senior politicians and the donors conspire to suppress any real sub-national experimentation if it appears to threaten their control over policy-making, as in the Niger 'extra pennies' experience, or their party-based powers, as in Malawi. This is ultimately about the way development 'policy' is viewed – too much as a token of right thinking that ensures access to budgetary and particularly donor-provided resources, too much as a source of cheap electoral gains, and too little as a means of achieving results on the ground.

The other theme of interest within an adaptive approach is the affinity which exists in practice between local problem-solving and what we have called practical hybridity: the willingness to construct institutions using the best available materials, marrying modern, professional knowledge and skills with ways of doing things successfully to which people are accustomed and which they understand. Thus, our third factor explaining outcomes, creating an environment that

---

1 See, notably, Korten (1980), Rondinelli (1983), Therkildsen (1988), Porter et al. (1991) and Mosse el al. (1998).

enhances the capacity of local people to solve their own problems, links up with the idea that there are advantages to 'working with the grain' of African societies (on which more below).

In summary, then, asking questions about maternal health and other public goods leads us back to fundamental questions about politics and aid – and not least to questions about the interaction between the two. Some of the biggest questions about politics are concerned with collective action problems at the elite level. Failure to resolve such problems at that level is the ultimate source of not only the reproduction of incoherent policy frameworks and the toleration of indiscipline in public goods provision, but also the inability to tolerate policy-making in the form of problem-solving from the bottom up.

A realistic take on collective action

Our overarching theme has been that support to development efforts in Africa needs to be reconceptualised as assistance to the solution of multilevel collective action problems. This means, as a first step, ceasing to rely on the easy assumption that bottom-up demand and the introduction of democratic processes can be relied upon as means of securing a development-oriented leadership and a well-performing public service. As we discussed in Chapter 4, the trappings of democracy do not guarantee the benefits that democracy provides, more or less effectively, in fully fledged capitalist economies that possess the sort of social class structure and institutions that capitalism generates. In societies where politics is a more lucrative and reliable source of livelihood than productive investment, multiparty political competition strengthens the tendency for policy-making to be driven by the needs of constructing and maintaining a supportive client base by allocating benefits in a discretionary way. It exaggerates a general tendency of democracy (Jacobs 2011) to focus political attention on tangible, short-term deliverables, not on the issues that matter for generating large, risky investments.

Further, in countries where there is little or no business community that is independent of state patronage, and where incumbent politicians can with impunity siphon off state resources for campaigning, the funding for opposition politics is going to be relatively weak. Oppositions will therefore crumble for lack of adequate resourcing if they do not fall apart for other reasons, such as ethnic fragmentation and incumbents' capacity to buy off opponents (Arriola 2013).

Incumbents will be able to act, therefore, as 'single parties in a multiparty setting'. Among other things, that will mean capturing service-delivery facilities, such as Malawi's water kiosks and market committees, for political purposes, adding to the challenges that local self-help initiatives already face.

The difficulties of initiating collective action were our focus in Chapter 5. While we think the collective action framework is a good framework for thinking about development generally, there are specific issues that deserve attention when it comes to sub-national arenas and local self-help. Here, solutions that work are locally anchored, meaning, we suggested, both that they are tailored to the specific details of the context (not generic, one-size-fits-all, remedies) and that they make efficient use of whatever already exists locally to serve such purposes – repertoires of institutional elements 'inherited from the past' or otherwise retained in the local culture.

The barriers to such solutions are of several types. They begin with the social fragmentation and resulting low levels of trust that exist in many developing-country settings, as exemplified by Ndirande, Malawi. One of the features of the transitional social structures that are typical in Africa is that they do not provide the luxury of socially homogeneous classes or status groups. While social homogeneity does not guarantee successful collective action, it surely helps. Problems such as the dangerous neglect of the Nasolo river in Blantyre are in principle soluble, but it is certain that they will not be solved so long as the problems of institutional incoherence in Blantyre's governance system and the problem of social fragmentation in Ndirande's population are not recognised and taken as the starting point of creative policy initiative – the sort of creativity that has been displayed, for example, in the reconstruction of local governance in Rwanda.

A second barrier lies in the limited appetite that current policy has for thinking in 'practical hybrid' terms. We have given several examples of initiatives that blend 'traditional' and modern elements with at least qualified success – the better examples of quasi-official local policing in Ndirande, Malawi, and Mwanza, Tanzania, and bwalo courts in Malawi. However, in all cases these are somewhat fragile arrangements, in some danger of being marginalised by 'modernising' impulses.

We also gave a brief account of two sectoral examples which have been more fully documented in APPP working papers. However, again both are the product of rather exceptional circumstances. First, the local justice service in Ghana that emerged as the most interesting example of practical hybridity in the comparative study done by Crook and colleagues was the mediation service of CHRAJ. CHRAJ was the product of the 1992 constitution-making process, one of the most creative moments in Ghana's modern history, and an event unlikely to be repeated. Secondly, the reforms to public schooling in Mali, Niger and Senegal studied by Villalón and Tidjani Alou are a response to one of the sharpest challenges to West African states in our time, that of reconciling secular governance arrangements with the preferences of Islamic majorities.

Releasing the potential of local problem-solving

In spite of everything, we have suggested, instances of local problem-solving and sub-national 'local reforms' do exist. However, these are distinct from the panaceas or magic bullets that have pre-occupied the development business during the good governance era: democratic decentralisation, client power and social accountability. These phrases identify institutional spheres within which solutions may be sought; they are not solutions in themselves.

Moreover, the relationship between locally anchored problem-solving and development aid is quite problematic. As we said at the beginning, a great deal of aid-funded effort is premised on false assumptions about how progress happens. Local problem-solving is about addressing the collective action problems that stakeholders face in specific local contexts. It calls for a high degree of sensitivity to possibly under-appreciated functions of existing arrangements as well as to the persistence of institutions that have outlived their usefulness (Ostrom et al. 2002; Corduneanu-Huci et al. 2013). As Bano (2012) has argued, injections of external funds can undermine existing collective action by destroying the institutional mechanisms that allow participants to have trust in their leaders. As other studies have shown, the imposition of generic organisational templates can interfere with genuine local problem-solving by discriminating against participants who do not know how to play the formal accountability game that the aid business requires.

There *are* ways that donors and NGOs can act more genuinely as development partners if they understand well the nature of these problems. Olivier de Sardan's 'discreet and responsive support to local reformers and to institutionalisation "from the bottom up"' (Olivier de Sardan 2012a) captures the general idea. The role of an embedded technical assistance agent in getting the 'extra pennies' initiative started may be a good example. Anyway, we are convinced that there are many more illustrations that could be given (although we have not been able to study them) of local NGOs and other organisations actually undertaking activities that we would characterise as facilitating solutions to local collective action problems. In many cases, they are being done under the auspices of project funding that is nominally about 'demand for good governance' or 'local accountability' – that is, based on a principal–agent diagnosis of the problem. Over the space of a few months, we noticed instances of this in grassroots interventions in Malawi, Sierra Leone and Tanzania (Booth 2012c).

We find this reassuring, especially in the context of other indications that leading international NGOs are redefining their role in terms of 'convening and brokering' – with the aim, in Duncan Green's words, 'not to build stuff, or dispense large amounts of cash, but to get disparate local players into a room and encourage them to find their own solutions' (Green 2012). To the extent that this is a trend that is already beginning to transform practice under the cover of social accountability and similar project funding, our appeal is for it to be given more explicit recognition by all concerned. If, on the ground, what is being done and what is working are convening and brokering, leading to some form of local collective action, the implementing organisations should be telling their funders about this. To the extent that this involves disturbing existing power relations, and is in this sense political, they should be saying that too. They should not be trying to force their reporting into a principal–agent straitjacket, even if the dictates of a renewal of funding and an appearance of being apolitical might make this the safest course of action. Above all, they should be documenting what they are doing, so that a better evidence base can be built up around what works and what does not.

A new reform agenda: making democracy safe for development

Our general plea in this book, about the need to overturn conventional principal–agent thinking, of whichever type, and embrace a diagnostic approach based in the theory of collective action, is addressed to a wide range of stakeholders in African development. Most importantly, we want African reformers and activists to hear our message and pass it on. At the same time, we want to address the big players in the international development business, from the World Bank to the official bilaterals and the new foundations. They do much to set the agenda, regionally and in each country.

For African reformers, there is little doubt that the top issue for practical follow-up is the dysfunctional relationship between the way national politics currently works and the needs of long-term development. We have argued that a fundamental issue is whether elites do or do not manage to resolve the collective action problems that prevent them from managing rents and running countries within a coordinated, long-term perspective. This challenge cannot be wished away by assuming either that democratic elections naturally give countries development-oriented leaders or that a bit of better-informed citizen pressure will do the trick. Under current African conditions, citizen pressure (as distinct from donor pressure mediated by NGOs) will normally lead to more effective clientelism, not better public policies. So the normal form of civil-society strengthening or 'democratic deepening' is not the solution.

Equally, however, the solution needs to be *about* democracy, if only because Africans have come to appreciate the civil rights that democratic openings have brought. The issue, then, is how to mitigate the most harmful economic and social impacts that multiparty political competition has under the kind of 'limited access order' that prevails in Africa. Chapter 5 of the Council on Foreign Relations book cited earlier (Halperin et al. 2010) is entitled 'Making development safe for democracy'. Without discounting the important issues discussed under that heading, we propose that it also needs to be looked at in reverse. The more immediate challenge is surely to make multiparty competitive politics more supportive of development.

There are several possible ingredients of a new fundamental agreement or political settlement. In ethnically divided societies, some element of power-sharing seems essential to take the heat out of the winner-takes-all and 'our turn to eat' syndromes. Power sharing is an important dimension of the political settlement that was forged in Rwanda between 2000 and 2003. The constitution of 2003 requires the winning presidential coalition to take no more than 50% of the cabinet posts, with the effect that eight of the ten legally registered political parties are involved in government (Golooba-Mutebi 2013). While this approach may have its downsides, it is undoubtedly one of the factors behind the remarkable level of policy stability and coherence that Rwanda has achieved over the last decade. Bigger and richer countries within the region would be wise to take note.

An alternative or complementary remedy would be an honest formulation of a shared national vision – an authentic Vision 2020 process rather than a token one – or at least a bargain among the main leadership contenders to ring-fence and exclude from current political competition and clientelist interference a small number of topics that are of vital importance for national development.

Such topics might include major infrastructure investments and their regulation, or food security and the challenging institutional arrangements needed to bring about the transformation of small-holder agriculture. Both rich and poor countries apply ring-fencing to monetary policy. Extending the same principle to other elements of macroeconomic stability and some top issues in development planning would have compelling advantages. The immediate costs to the current players may be less than imagined, meaning that the elite collective action problems involved in moving to such a position would be soluble in practice. At any rate, these are the kinds of issues that are central to the politics of economic transformation in twenty-first-century Africa. The gains from depoliticising them could be enormous.

A new aid agenda: facilitating complex change

The international assistance community may have only a modest role to play in getting acceptance of the kind of reform vision we have just proposed. It should, instead, expend its energies putting its own house in order – stopping doing things that evidently do not help and starting doing things that do. However, the critique of principal–agent, demand–supply thinking advanced in this book is relevant even to a limited agenda of self-reform. When, then, are the prospects for its adoption in mainstream aid thinking?

The obstacles to the uptake of such ideas at the technical level within the larger international agencies are relatively few. To be sure, tailoring assistance efforts to local contexts takes time and effort – much more time and effort than taking a standard solution off the shelf. Intellectually, many governance advisers and sector specialists within organisations like DfID have no problem with this. All that is at stake is the 'common-sense' ideology and simple morality that constantly feed the good-governance approach, and the more experienced agency staff already question these. They welcome the kind of challenge posed by this book. The downside, however, is that they work in organisational environments that give them powerful incentives *not* to do what intellectually they know is the right thing.

Development in Africa is hardly separable from the business of providing and securing external aid. This is less so in 2013 than it was in recent decades because of the new natural resource revenues to which governments are getting access and the availability of no-strings-attached finance from China and elsewhere. But this is only a relative shift. For some time yet, large and possibly increasing volumes of 'country programmable' aid are going to be available alongside donor contributions to multilateral agencies like the World Bank. Why? Because, for politicians in the North, being seen delivering assistance directly to poor countries is a relatively simple and risk-free means of showing that they care about global issues (Glennie 2008). It has political attractions that cannot be matched by international initiatives in areas like agricultural research, the arms trade, tax havens or narcotics policy, despite the evidence that success in these areas would have a greater positive impact (Moore et al. 2009; Brown et al. 2010).

This availability of funding for countries has incentive effects. It influences the internal workings of development agencies as well as the opportunity structures of individuals and organisations in aid recipient countries. So long as aid flows remain abundant, there will be pressures to disburse large sums on a more or less fixed timetable while minimising the 'administrative costs' of doing so, because voters have been told that development is essentially about transferring resources to poor people. Under these conditions, it is probably unrealistic to expect those designing new programmes to abandon the well-worn tracks created by previous generations of spending in such areas as general budget support, sector-wide approaches and public sector 'capacity development'. Even if the demonstrable gains from these past programmes are limited, disbursement targets encourage their renewal.

This context imparts a strong disincentive to anyone within a development agency proposing to devote time and effort to genuine institutional adaptation. Where, as in the UK currently, the international development budget is both expanding and contested politically, there is an additional factor. Programmes have to show measurable results within a few years, and do so on a predictable timetable. Otherwise, according to current understandings, they are not considered to represent 'value for money'. Yet facilitating complex change as advocated in this book is almost by definition a long-term and uncertain process, in which the gains are potentially far greater than those of conventional aid and governance support, but there are also risks. It is therefore hard to be sanguine about the possibilities for getting real uptake of our perspective on how to work more effectively on African governance among official donor agencies.

Even if it were possible to reduce the perverse effects of disbursement targets, there would remain a set of issues to do with the accountability requirements that are intrinsic to aid as a transfer funded by Northern taxpayers. This particularly affects the ability of agencies to accept what we have said about how not to support self-help at local levels. It is not realistic to expect Northern politicians to be unconcerned about accountability to their parliaments and taxpayers. Unfortunately, this implies that funding for community-based organisations and other local initiatives which uses aid money is highly likely to involve the imposition of rules and regulations which make it impossible for these organisations or initiatives to meet the conditions for genuine success.

In the final analysis, however, it is the aid business that has to change to meet the needs of development, not the other way round. Some recent evidence from the UK suggests that Northern voters may be more open to realistic accounts of how change happens and how aid can help in developing countries than political leaders suppose (Glennie et al. 2012). This poses a challenge to those international agencies that still recognise that they have duties in the field of development education, particularly those that in the past have advocated simplistic messages about the importance of money in eradicating global poverty. However, donor and NGO communicators cannot effect such a change in attitudes on their own. The challenge for the rest of us is to convince ministers, parliaments and the voting public in the North that reducing global poverty is more about power and institutions than about funding gaps.

We leave aside here the fact that globally the North under-regulates certain types of financial transactions and trade in ways that are systematically unfavourable to poverty-reduction efforts in the South. This case has been well made, and it deserves a wider hearing.

However, we have focused here on what happens at the country level in Africa, where differences in effort and performance under different types of political settlement are quite striking. Within countries, therefore, the point to be got across is that the prospects for successful economic and social transformation are largely about the fundamental political choices made and associated institutional solutions crafted by members of the national elite. Failures to construct political settlements that allow countries to realise their development potential and avoid dissipating that potential through large-scale corruption are invariably underpinned by unresolved elite-level collective action problems.

External assistance may have a limited role in facilitating change at this level, with some danger of producing perverse effects. The responsibilities of international powers with respect to national political settlements may need to be limited to 'doing no harm' (Putzel 2010) – that is, avoiding clumsy efforts to assist based on poor knowledge of realities on the ground. We have shown in this book, however, that there are opportunities for external actors to help in solving development problems and in facilitating the right sort of institutional change if they are really interested in doing so. The corresponding headline for Northern publics is that the diagnostic and design work that this entails is intensive in skilled labour and implies a real local presence in the country. Getting the right skills to the right places and in the right sectors for long enough is therefore one of the better uses of development assistance budgets, and should not be seen simply as an overhead cost.

Another idea that is strongly suggested by the APPP research and the arguments of this book is for more aid for development to be delivered by organisations that are not donor agencies. Working on institutions calls for serious local knowledge. It requires project designs that are adaptive – oriented to learning rather than the implementation of a blueprint – as Andrews et al. (2012) have reminded us. And it means being responsive to what country actors, in their moments of frankness, say they need, as opposed to what donors are able to provide or want to promote. There are serious doubts about whether official development agencies will ever achieve the quality of understanding and the management flexibility that this implies. As well as becoming less centred on delivering funds, therefore, the official agencies should probably be concerned to do more things 'at arm's length', delegating assistance to organisations that have demonstrated an ability to work in the ways that are required to make a positive difference.

Readers will have their own ideas about which organisations are actually or potentially suited to playing such a role. We have views as to which are the best current examples. We also think that recent governance programmes in Africa are beginning to generate some useful lessons about what works when an official donor tries to out-source the design and implementation of its governance-improvement portfolio. It is not automatic that there will be existing organisations equipped with the perspectives and skills to make a break with the conventions of 'good governance' and the demand-side principal–agent approach. However, these details properly belong to a future discussion.[2] What we want to establish first is the thought that aid may be better equipped to engage with the real problems of African governance if it is skilfully delivered at arm's length.

To readers who are broadly convinced by what we have had to say, we would propose that these are the things that should be at the centre of discussion over the coming years. Getting governance for development in Africa is about finding new ways of addressing collective action problems. This is going to entail a revolution in thinking around 'governance', not least within African countries. To the extent that outside support has a role in this, it entails a transformation in thinking about the proper use of aid budgets among politicians and voters in the North. More specifically, we would give priority to two practical steps. One is a robust commitment from the international NGO community to Duncan Green's 'convening and brokering' as opposed to 'delivering stuff'. The other is greater use of arm's-length assistance – funding of organisations that can do a better job of faciliating governance for development along the lines outlined here.

---

2 This is the focus of ongoing work in the Politics and Governance Programme and Centre for Aid and Public Expenditure at the Overseas Development Institute.

BIBLIOGRAPHY

APPP and DRA papers and policy briefs are generally downloadable from www.institutions-africa.org.

Ahmad, J., S. Devarajan, S. Khemani and S. Shah (2005) 'Decentralization and service delivery', Policy Research Working Paper 3603, Washington, DC: World Bank.

Anders, G. (2001) 'Freedom and insecurity: civil servants between support networks, the free market and the civil service reform', in H. Englund (ed.), *A Democracy of Chameleons: Politics and Culture in the New Malawi*, Uppsala: Nordiska Afrikain-institutet, pp. 43–61.

— (2009) 'Like chameleons: civil servants and corruption in Malawi', in G. Blundo and P.-Y. Le Meur (eds), *The Governance of Daily Life in Africa: Public and Collective Services and Their Users*, Leiden: Brill, pp. 119–42.

Andersson, K. P., C. C. Gibson and F. Lehoucq (2004) 'The politics of decentralized natural resource governance', *PS: Political Science and Politics*, 37(3): 421–6.

Andrews, M. (2008) 'The good governance agenda: beyond indicators without theory', *Oxford Development Studies*, 36(4): 379–407.

Andrews, M., L. Pritchett and M. Wool-cock (2012) 'Escaping capability traps through Problem-Driven Iterative Adaptation (PDIA)', Working Paper 299, Washington, DC: Center for Global Development.

APPP, Developmental Leadership Programme, Elites Production and Poverty, Political Economy of Agri-cultural Policy in Africa and Tracking Development (2012) *The Political Economy of Development in Africa: A Joint Statement from Five Research Programmes*, Copenhagen: Danish Institute of International Studies, differenttakeonafrica.files.wordpress.com/2012/04/joint-statement.pdf.

ARD Inc. (2010) *Comparative Assessment of Decentralization in Africa: Final Report and Summary of Findings*, Washington, DC: USAID.

Arriola, L. R. (2013) *Multiethnic Co-alitions in Africa: Business Funancing of Opposition Election Campaigns*, Cambridge: Cambridge University Press.

Autesserre, S. (2010) *The Trouble with the Congo: Local Violence and the Failure of International Peacebuilding*, Cambridge: Cambridge University Press.

Bano, M. (2012) *Breakdown in Pakistan: How Aid is Eroding Institutions for Collective Action*, Stanford, CA: Stanford University Press.

Bardhan, P. (2005) 'Decentralization of governance', in P. Bardhan (ed.), *Scarcity, Conflicts, and Cooperation: Essays in the Political and Institutional Economics of Development*, Cambridge, MA: MIT Press, pp. 105–27.

Bates, R. H. (1981) *Markets and States in Tropical Africa: The Political Basis of Agricultural Policies*, Berkeley: University of California Press.

Batley, R. and G. A. Larbi (2005) 'Capacity to deliver? Management, institutions and public services in developing countries', in Y. Bangura and G. A. Larbi (eds), *Public Sector Reform in Developing Countries:*

Capacity Challenges to Improve Services, London: Palgrave Macmillan/ UNRISD, pp. 99–127.

Becker, F. (2009) '"Bad governance" and the persistence of alternative political arenas: a study of a Tanzanian region', in G. Blundo and P.-Y. Le Meur (eds), *The Governance of Daily Life in Africa: Ethnographic Explorations of Public and Collective Services*, Leiden: Brill, pp. 73–99.

Bierschenk, T. and J.-P. Olivier de Sardan (2003) 'Powers in the village: rural Benin between democratisation and decentralisation', *Africa*, 73(2): 145–73.

Blundo, G. (1998) 'Decentralisation, participation and corruption in Senegal', Paper presented at the 14th International Congress of Anthropological and Ethnological Sciences, Williamsburg, VA.

— (2006) 'Dealing with the local state: the informal privatization of street-level bureaucracies in Senegal', *Development and Change*, 37(4): 799–819.

— (2009) 'Des ordures et des hommes: la gouvernance de l'assainissement à Dogondoutchi', in J.-P. Olivier de Sardan and M. Tidjani Alou (eds), *Les pouvoirs locaux au Niger, Tome 1: À la veille de la décentralisation*, Dakar and Paris: CODESRIA/Karthala, pp. 113–50.

— (2011a) '"Comme un ballon de foot": La gestion quotidienne des resources humaines dans les services forestiers en Afrique de l'Ouest', in P.-Y. Le Meur, N. Shareika and E. Spies (eds), *Ethnologie auf dem Boden der Tatsachen: Festschrift für Thomad Bierschenk*, Cologne: Rüdiger Köppe Verlag.

— (2011b) 'Une administration à deux vitesses: projets de développement et construction de l'État au Sahel', *Cahiers d'Études Africaines*, 202/203: 427–52.

— (2012) 'Le roi n'est pas un parent: Les multiples redevabilités au sein de l'Etat postcolonial en Afrique', in P. Haag and C. Lemieux (eds), *Faire des sciences sociales: Critiquer*, Paris: Editions de l'EHESS, pp. 59–86.

— (forthcoming) 'Bureaucratic culture and local reforms in West Africa Forest Services', in T. Bierschenk and J.-P. Olivier de Sardan (eds), *States at Work in West Africa*, Leiden: Brill.

Blundo, G. and P.-Y. Le Meur (eds) (2008) *The Governance of Daily Life in Africa: Ethnographic Explorations of Public and Collective Services*, Leiden: Brill.

Blundo, G. and J.-P. Olivier de Sardan, with N. B. Arifari and M. T. Alou (2006) *Everyday Corruption and the State: Citizens and Public Officials in Africa*, London: Zed Books.

— (eds) (2007) *État et corruption en Afrique: Une anthropologie comparative des relations entre fonctionnaires et usagers (Bénin, Niger, Sénégal)*, Marseille and Paris: APAD/Karthala.

Bonfiglio, A. (2003) *Empowering the Poor: Local Governance for Poverty Reduction*, New York: United Nations Capital Development Fund.

Booth, D. (2011) *Governance for Development in Africa: Building on What Works*, Policy Brief 01, London: Africa Power and Politics Programme.

— (2012a) *Development as a Collective Action Problem: Addressing the Real Challenges of African Governance*, London: ODI/Africa Power and Politics.

— (2012b) 'Working with the grain and swimming against the tide: barriers to uptake of research findings on governance and public services in low-income Africa', *Public Management Review*, 14(2): 163–80.

— (2012c) 'The centrality of collective action problems in governance for development: new evidence', in *Goverance for Development*, Washington, DC: World Bank, blogs. worldbank.org/governance, accessed 25 October 2012.

Booth, D. and F. Golooba-Mutebi (2009) 'Aiding economic growth in Africa: the political economy of roads reform in Uganda', Working Paper 307, London: Overseas Development Institute.

— (2012) 'Developmental patrimonialism? The case of Rwanda', *African Affairs*, 111(444): 379–403.

Booth, D., D. Cammack, J. Harrigan, E. Kanyongolo, M. Mataure and N. Ngwira (2006) 'Drivers of change and development in Malawi', Working Paper 261, London: Overseas Development Institute.

Brett, E. A. (2003) 'Participation and accountability in development management', *Journal of Development Studies*, 40(2): 1–29.

— (2012) 'Problematising the democratic imperative: the challenge of transition and consolidation in weak states', Draft paper, London School of Economics.

Brown, T., S. Unsworth and G. Williams (2010) 'Addressing the international drivers of corruption at the country level', Oxford and Bristol: The Policy Practice and IDL Group.

Cameron, D. (2012) 'Combating poverty at its roots: economic development requires aid, but also sound institutions', *Wall Street Journal Online*, online.wsj.com/article, 1 November.

Cammack, D. (2012a) 'Peri-urban governance and the delivery of public goods in Malawi, 2009–11', Research Report 03, London: Africa Power and Politics Programme.

— (2012b) 'Malawi in crisis, 2011–12', *Review of African Political Economy*, 39(132): 375–88.

Cammack, D. and E. Kanyongolo (2010) 'Local governance and public goods in Malawi', Working Paper 11, London: Africa Power and Politics Programme.

Cammack, D. and T. Kelsall, with D. Booth (2010) 'Developmental patrimonialism? The case of Malawi', Working Paper 12, London: Africa Power and Politics Programme.

Cammack, D., E. Kanyongolo and T. O'Neil (2009) '"Town chiefs" in Malawi', Working Paper 3, London: Africa Power and Politics Programme.

Cammack, D., F. Golooba-Mutebi, F. Kanyongolo and T. O'Neil (2007) 'Neopatrimonial politics, decentralisation and local government: Uganda and Malawi in 2006', Good Governance, Aid Modalities and Poverty Reduction Working Paper 2, London: Overseas Development Institute.

Chabal, P. and J.-P. Daloz (2006) *Culture Troubles: Politics and the Interpretation of Meaning*, London: Hurst.

Chambers, V. (2012) *Improving Maternal Health When Resources are Limited: Safe Motherhood in Rural Rwanda*, Policy Brief 05, London: Africa Power and Politics Programme.

Chambers, V. and F. Golooba-Mutebi (2012) 'Is the bride too beautiful? Safe motherhood in rural Rwanda', Research Report 04, London: Africa Power and Politics Programme.

Chang, H.-J. (2002) *Kicking Away the Ladder: Development Strategy in Historical Perspective*, London: Anthem Press.

— (ed.) (2007a) *Institutional Change and Economic Development*, London: Anthem Press/UN University Press.

— (2007b) 'Understanding the relationship between institutions and economic development: some key theoretical issues', in H.-J. Chang (ed.), *Institutional Change and Economic Development*, London: Anthem Press/UN University Press, pp. 17–33.

Chuhan-Pole, P. and M. Angwafo (eds) (2011) *Yes Africa Can: Success Stories from a Dynamic Continent*, Washington, DC: World Bank.

Cissokho, S. (2012) 'Le transport à deux vitesses: Informalisation et privatisation du service public des gares routières au Sénégal', Background Paper 12, London: Africa Power and Politics Programme.

Citizenship DRC (2011) *Blurring the Boundaries: Citizen Action across States and Societies*, Brighton: Citizenship, Participation and Accountability Development Research Centre.

Clemens, M. A., C. J. Kenny and T. J. Moss (2007) 'The trouble with the MDGs: confronting expectations of aid and development success', *World Development*, 35(5): 735–51.

Collier, P. (2007) *The Bottom Billion: Why the Poorest Countries are Failing and What Can be Done about It*, Oxford: Oxford University Press.

Connerley, E. F., K. Eaton and P. Smoke (eds) (2010) *Making Decentralization Work: Democracy, Development, and Security*, Boulder, CO: Lynne Rienner.

Cooksey, B. and T. Kelsall (2011) 'The political economy of the investment climate in Tanzania', Research Report 01, London: Africa Power and Politics Programme.

Corduneanu-Huci, C., A. Hamilton and I. Masses Ferrer (2013) *Understanding Policy Change: How to Apply Political Economy Concepts in Practice*, Washington, DC: World Bank.

Crawford, G. and C. Hartmann (eds) (2008) *Decentralisation in Africa: A Pathway out of Poverty and Conflict?*, Amsterdam: Amsterdam University Press.

Crook, R. C. (2010) 'Rethinking civil service reform in Africa: "islands of effectiveness" and organisational commitment', *Commonwealth and Comparative Politics*, 48(4): 479–504.

— (2011) *The State and Accessible Justice in Africa: is Ghana Unique?*, Policy Brief 03, London: Africa Power and Politics Programme.

— (2012) 'Alternative dispute resolution and the magistrate's courts in Ghana: a case of practical hybridity', Working Paper 25, London: Africa Power and Politics Programme.

Crook, R. C. and D. Booth (eds) (2011) 'Working with the grain? Rethinking African governance', *IDS Bulletin*, 42(2).

Crook, R. C. and J. Manor (1998) *Democracy and Decentralisation in South Asia and West Africa: Participation, Accountability and Performance*, Cambridge: Cambridge University Press.

Crook, R. C. and A. S. Sverrisson (2003) 'Does decentralization contribute to poverty reduction? Surveying the evidence', in P. P. Houtzager and M. Moore (eds), *Changing Paths: International Development and the New Politics of Inclusion*, Ann Arbor: University of Michigan Press, pp. 233–59.

Crook, R., K. Asante and V. Brobbey (2010) 'Popular concepts of justice and fairness in Ghana: testing the legitimacy of new or hybrid forms of state justice', Working Paper 14, London: Africa Power and Politics Programme.

Cross, C. (2011) 'Community policing in Tanzania: from *sungusungu* to *polisi jamii*', Paper presented at the EADI/DSA General Conference, University of York, 19–22 September.

Devarajan, S., S. Khemani and M. Walton (2011) 'Civil society, public action and accountability in Africa', Policy Research Working Paper 5733, Washington, DC: World Bank.

DfID (2009) *Political Economy Analysis How to Note*, London: Department for International Development.

Diarra, A. (2009) 'La prise en charge de l'accouchement dans trois communes au Niger: Say, Balleyara et Guidan Roumji', Field report, Niamey: LASDEL.

— (2011) 'La mise en oeuvre de la politique d'exemption de paiement dans les districts sanitaires de Gaweye et de Say', *Etudes et Travaux*, 96, Niamey: LASDEL.

Dill, B. (2009) 'The paradoxes of community-based participation in Dar es Salaam', *Development and Change*, 40(4): 717–43.

— (2010) 'Community-Based Organizations (CBOs) and norms of participation in Tanzania: working against the grain', *African Studies Review*, 53(2): 23–48.

Doucouliagos, H. and M. A. Ulubasoglu (2008) 'Democracy and economic growth: a meta-analysis', *American Journal of Political Science*, 52(1): 61–83.

Eaton, K., K. Kaiser and P. Smoke (2010) *The Political Economy of Decentralization Reforms: Implications for Aid Effectiveness*, Washington, DC: World Bank.

Evans, P. B. (2004) 'Development as institutional change: the pitfalls of monocropping and the potentials of deliberation', *Studies in Comparative International Development*, 38(4): 30–52.

Faust, J. (2010) 'Policy experiments, democratic ownership and development assistance', *Development Policy Review*, 28(5): 515–34.

Fjeldstad, O.-H. and O. Therkildsen (2008) 'Mass taxation and state–society relations in East Africa', in D. Bräutigam, O.-H. Fjeldstad and M. Moore (eds), *Taxation and State-building in Developing Countries: Capacity and Consent*, Cambridge: Cambridge University Press, pp. 114–34.

Fritz, V., K. Kaiser and B. Levy (2009) *Problem-driven Governance and Political Economy Analysis: Good Practice Framework*, Washington, DC: World Bank, PREM Network.

Fukuyama, F. (2004) *State-building: Governance and World Order in the Twenty-first Century*, London: Profile Books.

Future State, Centre for the (2005) *Signposts to More Effective States: Responding to Governance Challenges in Developing Countries*, Brighton: Institute of Development Studies.

— (2010) *An Upside Down View of Governance*, Brighton: Institute of Development Studies.

Gaventa, J. and R. McGee (eds) (2010) *Citizen Action and National Policy Reform: Making Change Happen*, London: Zed Books.

Geddes, B. (1994) *Politician's Dilemma: Building State Capacity in Latin America*, Berkeley: University of California Press.

Gerring, J., P. Kingstone, M. Lange and A. Sinha (2011) 'Democracy, history, and economic performance: a case-study approach', *World Development*, 39(10): 1735–48.

Gibson, C. C., K. Andersson, E. Ostrom and S. Shivakumar (2005) *The Samaritan's Dilemma: The Political Economy of Development Aid*, Oxford: Oxford University Press.

Glennie, A., W. Straw and L. Wild (2012) *Understanding Public Attitudes to Aid and Development*, London: Institute of Public Policy Research/Overseas Development Institute.

Glennie, J. (2008) *The Trouble with Aid: Why Less Could Mean More for Africa*, London: Zed Books.

Global Forum on Local Development (2010) *Pursuing the MDGs through Local Government*, New York: United Nations Capital Development Fund.

Goetz, A. M., J. Gaventa and associates

(2001) 'Bringing citizen voice and client focus into service delivery', Working Paper 138, Brighton: Institute of Development Studies.

Golooba-Mutebi, F. (2005) 'When popular participation won't improve service provision: primary health care in Uganda', *Development Policy Review*, 23(2): 165–82.

— (2007) 'Chiefs, politicians, and the community in Uganda: a historico-analytical narrative', Paper presented at the 4th National Annual Local Government Conference, Durban, South Africa.

— (2008) 'Background: governance in Uganda', in *Katine: It Starts with a Village*, www.guardian.co.uk/katine/2008/mar/06/katinegoalbackground.background3, accessed 13 July 2009.

— (2011) 'Maternal health delivery in Rwanda and Uganda: exploring sources of success and failure', Paper presented at the EADI/DSA Conference, York, 19–22 September.

— (2013) 'Kagame's no dictator, I have his permission to say so', *East African* (Nairobi), 9–15 February, p. 19.

— (forthcoming) 'Maternal health services in Uganda: exploring sources of success and failure', Working paper, London: Africa Power and Politics Programme.

Golooba-Mutebi, F., J. B. Mubiru, D. Bataringaya, A. Nannungi and B. Sabiti (2011) 'Maternal health in Rakai District (field report)', London: Africa Power and Politics Programme.

Gómez-Temesio, V. (2010) 'Régulation des marchés et assainissement de l'eau au Senegal: Rapport de l'enquête initiée en novembre 2009', Paper presented at the APPP Local Governance Workshop, Paris.

Government of Malawi (2005) *National Water Policy*, Lilongwe: Ministry of Irrigation and Water Development.

Green, D. (2012) 'What have we learned from 5 years of research on African power and politics?', in *From Poverty to Power*, www.oxfamblogs.org/fp2p/?p=12453, accessed 12 November 2012.

Greif, A. (2006) *Institutions and the Path to the Modern Economy: Lessons from Medieval Trade*, Cambridge: Cambridge University Press.

Grindle, M. (2004) 'Good enough governance: poverty reduction and reform in developing countries', *Governance: An International Journal of Policy, Administration, and Institutions*, 17(4): 525–48.

— (2007) 'Good enough governance revisited', *Development Policy Review*, 25(5): 553–74.

— (2011) 'Governance reform: the new analytics of next steps', *Governance*, 24(3): 415–18.

Gugerty, M. K. and M. Kremer (2008) 'Outside funding and the dynamics of participation in community associations', *American Journal of Political Science*, 52(3): 585–602.

Habyarimana, J., M. Humphreys, D. N. Posner and J. M. Weinstein (2007) 'Why does ethnic diversity undermine public goods provision?', *American Political Science Review*, 101(4): 709–25.

— (2009) *Coethnicity: Diversity and the Dilemmas of Collective Action*, New York: Russell Sage Foundation.

Halperin, M. H., J. T. Siegle and M. M. Weinstein (2010) *The Democracy Advantage: How Democracies Promote Prosperity and Peace*, revised edn, New York: Routledge/Council on Foreign Relations.

Hardin, R. (1982) *Collective Action*, Baltimore, MD: Johns Hopkins University Press.

Henley, D. and J. K. van Donge (2012) *Policy for Development in Africa: Learning from What Worked in Southeast Asia*, Policy Brief 01, London: Developmental Regimes in Africa Project.

Houtzager, P. P., A. Joshi and A. G. Lavalle (eds) (2008) 'State reform and social accountability: Brazil, India and Mexico', *IDS Bulletin*, 38(6).

Hyden, G. (2010) 'Political accountability in Africa: is the glass half-full or half-empty?', Working Paper 6, London: Africa Power and Politics Programme.

Hyden, G. and M. Mmuya (2008) 'Power and policy slippage in Tanzania: discussing national ownership of development', *Sida Studies*, Stockholm: Sida.

Igoe, J. (2003) 'Scaling up civil society: donor money, NGOs and the pastoralist land rights movement in Tanzania', *Development and Change*, 34(5): 863–85.

Issa, Y. (2011) 'Le service public de l'eau et de l'assainissement à Say, Guidan Roumdji et Balleyara', Etudes et Travaux/Background Paper 93/13, Niamey and London: LASDEL/APPP.

Jacobs, A. M. (2011) *Governing for the Long Term: Democracy and the Politics of Investment*, Cambridge: Cambridge University Press.

Joshi, A. (2007) 'When do the poor demand better services? Accountability, responsiveness and collective action in service delivery', in S. Devarajan and I. Widlund (eds), *The Politics of Service Delivery in Democracies: Better Access for the Poor*, Stockholm: Ministry of Foreign Affairs/EGDI, pp. 70–84.

Joshi, A. and J. Ayee (2008) 'Associational taxation: a pathway into the informal sector?', in D. Bräutigam, O.-H. Fjeldstad and M. Moore (eds), *Taxation and State-building in Developing Countries: Capacity and Consent*, Cambridge: Cambridge University Press, pp. 183–211.

Joshi, A. and P. P. Houtzager (2012) 'Widgets or watchdogs? Conceptual explorations in social accountability', *Public Management Review*, 14(2): 145–62.

Joshi, A. and M. Moore (2004) 'Institutionalised co-production: unorthodox public service delivery in challenging environments', *Journal of Development Studies*, 40(4): 31–41.

Jütting, J., E. Corsi, C. Kauffmann, I. McDonnell, H. Osterrieder, N. Pinaud and L. Wegner (2005) 'What makes decentralisation in developing countries pro-poor?', *European Journal of Development Research*, 17(4): 626–48.

Kafando, Y., B. Mazou, S. Kouanda and V. Ridde (2011) 'Les retards de remboursements liés à la politique de gratuité des soins au Niger ont des effets néfastes sur la capacité financière des formations sanitaires', *Etudes et Travaux*, 99, Niamey: LASDEL.

Kaplan, S. D. (2008) *Fixing Fragile States: A New Paradigm for Development*, Westport, CT: Praeger.

Kayizzi-Mugerwa, S. (ed.) (2003) *Reforming Africa's Institutions: Ownership, Incentives, and Capabilities*, Tokyo: United Nations University Press/ WIDER.

Keefer, P. (2007) 'Clientelism, credibility, and the policy choices of young democracies', *American Journal of Political Science*, 51(4): 804–21.

Keefer, P. and S. Khemani (2005) 'Democracy, public expenditures, and the poor: understanding political incentives for providing public services', *World Bank Research Observer*, 20(1): 1–27.

Keefer, P. and S. Wolters (2011) 'Democratic Republic of Congo: citizen and elite fragmentation and the political economy of growth', Draft working paper, Washington, DC: World Bank.

Kelsall, T. (2004) 'Contentious politics, local governance and the self: a Tanzanian case study', Research Report 129, Uppsala: Nordiska Afrikainstitutet.

— (2008a) 'Public goods, collective action and case study design: a think piece using Tanzanian materials for the local leadership strand of APPP', APPP unpublished paper, Phnom Penh.

— (2008b) 'Going with the grain in African development?', *Development Policy Review*, 26(6): 627–55.

— (2009) 'Game-theoretic models, social mechanisms and public goods in Africa: a methodological discussion', Discussion Paper 7, London: Africa Power and Politics Programme.

— (2013) *Business, Politics, and the State in Africa: Challenging the Orthodoxies on Growth and Transformation*, London: Zed Books.

Kelsall, T. and D. Booth, with D. Cammack and F. Golooba-Mutebi (2010) 'Developmental patrimonialism? Questioning the orthodoxy on political governance and economic progress in Africa', Working Paper 9, London: Africa Power and Politics Programme.

Kelsall, T., S. Lange, S. Mesaki and M. Mmuya (2005) *Understanding Patterns of Accountability in Tanzania: Component 2 – the Bottom-Up Perspective*, Oxford: Oxford Policy Management/Christian Michelsen Institute/REPOA.

Kenny, C. (2005) 'Why are we worried about income? Nearly everything that matters is converging', *World Development*, 33(1): 1–19.

Khan, M. (1995) 'State failure in weak states: a critique of new institutionalist explanations', in J. Harriss, J. Hunter and C. M. Lewis (eds), *The New Institutional Economics and Third World Development*, London: Routledge, pp. 71–86.

— (2007) 'Governance, economic growth and development since the 1960s', in J. A. Ocampo, K. S. Jomo and R. Vos (eds), *Growth Divergences: Explaining Differences in Economic Performance*, London: Zed Books/United Nations, pp. 285–323.

— (2010) *Political Settlements and the Governance of Growth-enhancing Institutions*, London: Economics Department, School of Oriental and African Studies, University of London.

Kjaer, A. M. and M. Katusiimeh (2012) 'Growing but not transforming: fragmented ruling coalitions and economic developments in Uganda', DIIS/EPP Working Paper 2012:07, Copenhagen: Danish Institute for International Studies.

Kjaer, A. M. and O. Therkildsen (2011) *Elections in Africa: Mixed Blessings for Growth and Poverty Alleviation*, Policy Brief, Copenhagen: Danish Institute for International Studies/Elites Production and Poverty Programme.

Korten, D. C. (1980) 'Community organization and rural development: a learning process approach', *Public Administration Review*, 40(5): 480–511.

Lange, S. (2008) 'The depoliticisation of development and the democratisation of politics in Tanzania: parallel structures as obstacles to delivering services to the poor', *Journal of Development Studies*, 44(8): 1122–44.

Lawson, A. and L. Rakner (2005) 'Understanding patterns of accountability in Tanzania: final synthesis report', Oxford: OPM/CMA/REPOA.

Leftwich, A. (2000) *States of Development: On the Primacy of Politics in Development*, Cambridge: Polity Press.

Leftwich, A. and C. Wheeler (2011) *Politics, Leadership and Coalitions in*

Development: A Research and Policy Workshop Report, Developmental Leadership Program, www.dlprog. org.

Leinweber, A. (2012a) 'Muslim schools in post-conflict D.R. Congo: new hybrid institutions in a weak state', Working Paper 22, London: Africa Power and Politics Programme.

— (2012b) 'The Muslim minority of the Democratic Republic of Congo, from historic marginalization and internal division to collective action', Cahiers d'Études Africaines, 2006/07: 517–44.

Leonard, D. (2010) '"Pockets" of effective agencies in weak governance states: where are they likely and why does it matter?', Public Administration and Development, 30: 91–101.

Leonard, D. K. (2000) Africa's Changing Markets for Health and Veterinary Services: The New Institutional Issues, New York: St Martin's Press.

Levy, B. (2004) 'Governance and economic development in Africa: meeting the challenge of capacity building', in B. Levy and S. Kpundeh (eds), Building State Capacity in Africa: New Approaches, Emerging Lessons, Washington, DC: World Bank/World Bank Institute, pp. 1–42.

— (2011) 'Can islands of effectiveness thrive in difficult governance settings? The political economy of local-level collaborative governance', Policy Reseach Working Paper 5842, Washington, DC: World Bank.

Levy, B. and S. Kpundeh (eds) (2004) Building State Capacity in Africa: New Approaches, Emerging Lessons, Washington, DC: World Bank.

Lindberg, S. I. (2009) 'Member of Parliament in Ghana: a hybrid institution with mixed effects', Working Paper 2, London: Africa Power and Politics Programme.

Lindemann, S. (2008) 'Do inclusive elite bargains matter? A research frame-work for understanding the causes of civil war in sub-Saharan Africa', Discussion Paper 15, London: Crisis States Research Centre, London School of Economics.

Lipsey, R. G. and K. Lancaster (1956) 'The general theory of second-best', Review of Economic Studies, 24(1): 11–32.

Malena, C., with R. Forster and J. Singh (2004) 'Social accountability: an introduction to the concept and emerging practice', Social Development Papers 76, Washington, DC: World Bank.

Manor, J. (2007) 'Introduction: synthesizing case study findings', in J. Manor (ed.), Aid that Works: Successful Development in Fragile States, Washington, DC: World Bank, pp. 1–36.

Mansuri, G. and V. Rao (2012) Localizing Development: Does Participation Work?, Washington, DC: World Bank.

McGee, R. and J. Gaventa (2010) 'Review of impact and effectiveness of transparency and accountability initiatives: synthesis report', Brighton: Institute of Development Studies.

McKinsey Global Institute (2010) Lions on the Move: The Progress and Potential of African Economies, Washington, DC: McKinsey & Co.

McNeil, M. and C. Malena (eds) (2010) Demanding Good Governance: Lessons from Social Accountability Initiatives in Africa, Washington, DC: World Bank.

Miguel, E. (2004) 'Tribe or nation? Nation building and public goods in Kenya versus Tanzania', World Politics, 56: 327–62.

Miguel, E. and M. K. Gugerty (2005) 'Ethnic diversity, social sanctions, and public goods in Kenya', Journal of Public Economics, 89: 2325–68.

Mills, G. and J. Herbst (2012) Africa's Third Liberation: The New Search for Prosperity and Jobs, Johannesburg: Penguin Books.

MINECOFIN (2006) 'Aid policy', Kigali: Ministry of Finance and Economic Planning, Government of Rwanda.

Mockus, A. (2005) 'Ampliación de los modos de hacer política', Paper presented at the Colloque CERI, 'La démocratie en Amérique latine: un renouvellement du personnel politique', Paris, 2/3 December 2004, www.ceri-sciences-po.org.

Moore, M., A. Schmidt and S. Unsworth (2009) 'Assuring our common future in a globalised world: the global context of conflict and state fragility', Brighton: Institute of Development Studies.

Mosse, D., J. Farrington and A. Rew (eds) (1998) *Development as Process: Concepts and Methods for Working with Complexity*, London: Routledge.

Ndegwa, S. N. and B. Levy (2004) 'The politics of decentralization in Africa: a comparative analysis', in B. Levy and S. Kpundeh (eds), *Building State Capacity in Africa: New Approaches, Emerging Lessons*, Washington, DC: World Bank/World Bank Institute, pp. 283–321.

NISR, Ministry of Health and ICF International (2012) *Rwanda Demographic and Health Survey 2010: Final Report*, Kigali: National Institute of Statistics of Rwanda.

Njamwea, M. M. (2003) 'Upgrading informal settlements by securing public spaces: case study of informal settlements in Blantyre City, Malawi', MSc thesis, International Institute for Geo-Information Science and Earth Observation, University of Twente, Netherlands.

Noman, A., K. Botchwey, H. Stein and J. E. Stiglitz (eds) (2012) *Good Growth and Governance in Africa: Rethinking Development Strategies*, Oxford: Oxford University Press.

North, D. C., J. J. Wallis and B. R. Weingast (2009) *Violence and Social Orders: A Conceptual Framework for Interpreting Recorded Human History*, Cambridge: Cambridge University Press.

— (eds) (2013) *In the Shadow of Violence: Politics, Economics, and the Problems of Development*, Cambridge: Cambridge University Press.

Nussbaum, B. (2003) 'African culture and ubuntu: reflections of a South African in America', *World Business Academy*, 17(1): 1–12.

O'Neil, T., M. Foresti and A. Hudson (2007) *Evaluation of Citizens' Voice and Accountability: Review of the Literature and Donor Approaches*, London: DfID.

ODI/TPP (recurrent) 'Political economy analysis in action: a training course for DfID, GIZ, Irish Aid and UNDP', London: Overseas Development Institute and The Policy Practice.

Odugbemi, S. and T. Jacobson (eds) (2008) *Governance Reform under Real-world Conditions: Citizens, Stakeholders, and Voice*, Washington, DC: World Bank.

Olivier de Sardan, J.-P. (1999) 'A Moral economy of corruption in Africa?', *Journal of Modern African Studies*, 37(1): 25–52.

— (2008a) 'State bureaucracy and governance in francophone West Africa: an empirical diagnosis and historical perspective', in G. Blundo (ed.), *The Governance of Everyday Life in Africa: Ethnographic Explorations of Public and Collective Services*, Leiden: Brill, pp. 39–71.

— (2008b) 'Researching the practical norms of real governance in Africa', Discussion Paper 5, London: Africa Power and Politics Programme.

— (2009a) 'Development, governance and reforms: studying practical norms in the delivery of public goods and services', in C. Widmark and S. Hagberg (eds), *Ethnographic*

Practice and Public Aid: Methods and Meaning in Development Cooperation, Uppsala: Acta Universitatis Upsaliensis, pp. 101–23.

— (2009b) 'The eight modes of local governance in West Africa', Working Paper 4, London: Africa Power and Politics Programme.

— (2012a) *Providing Public Goods: Local Responses to Policy Incoherence and State Failure in Niger*, Policy Brief 04, London: Africa Power and Politics Programme.

— (2012b) 'Local governance: the delivery of four public goods in three municipalities of Niger (Phase 2 synthesis)', Working Paper 21, London: Africa Power and Politics Programme.

Olivier de Sardan, J.-P., with A. Abdulkader, A. Diarra, Y. Issa, H. Moussa, A. Oumarou and M. T. Alou (2010a) 'Local governance and public goods in Niger', Working Paper 10, London: Africa Power and Politics Programme.

Olivier de Sardan, J.-P., V. Ridde, A. Diarra and A. Ousseini (2010b) 'Pour une réflexion sur la gratuité des soins au Niger', Programme 'Abolition du paiement', Note d'information 1, Niamey: LASDEL.

Olowu, D. (2006) 'Decentralization policies and practices under structural adjustment and democratization in Africa', in Y. Bangura and G. A. Larbi (eds), *Public Sector Reform in Developing Countries: Capacity Challenges to Improve Services*, London: Palgrave Macmillan/UNRISD, pp. 228–54.

Olson, M. (1965) *The Logic of Collective Action: Public Goods and the Theory of Groups*, Cambridge, MA: Harvard University Press.

Ostrom, E. (1990) *Governing the Commons: The Evolution of Institutions for Collective Action*, Cambridge: Cambridge University Press.

— (2005) *Understanding Institutional Diversity*, Princeton, NJ: Princeton University Press.

Ostrom, E., T. Dietz, N. Dolšak, P. C. Stern, S. Stonich and E. U. Weber (eds) (2002) *The Drama of the Commons*, Washington, DC: National Academy Press.

Oumarou, A. (2011) 'Le service public de marché à Balleyara, Guidan Roumdji et Say', Etudes et Travaux/Background Paper 90/15, Niamey and London: LASDEL/APPP.

Persson, A., B. Rothstein and J. Teorell (2010) 'The failure of anti-corruption policies: a theoretical mischaracterization of the problem', QoG Working Paper 2010:19, Gothenburg: Quality of Government Institute, University of Gothenburg.

Poole, A. (2011) 'Political economy assessments at sector and project levels', Washington, DC: World Bank, Political Economy Community of Practice/GAC in Projects.

Porter, D., B. Allen and G. Thompson (1991) *Development in Practice: Paved with Good Intentions*, London: Routledge.

Posner, D. N. (2005) *Institutions and Ethnic Politics in Africa*, Cambridge: Cambridge University Press.

Poteete, A. R. and J. C. Ribot (2011) 'Repertoires of domination: decentralization as process in Botswana and Senegal', *World Development*, 39(3): 439–49.

Poulton, C. (2011) 'Democratization and the political economy of agricultural policy in Africa', Paper presented at the African Studies Association, Washington, DC, 17–19 November.

Pritchett, L. and M. Woolcock (2008) 'Solutions when the solution is the problem: arraying the disarray in development', in W. Easterly (ed.), *Reinventing Foreign Aid*, Cambridge, MA: MIT Press, pp. 147–77.

Pritchett, L., M. Woolcock and M. Andrews (2010) 'Capability traps? The mechanisms of persistent implementation failure', Working Paper 234, Washington, DC: Center for Global Development.

Putzel, J. (2010) *Do No Harm: International Support for Statebuilding*, Paris: OECD DAC Fragile State Group.

Radelet, S. (2010) *Emerging Africa: How 17 Countries are Leading the Way*, Washington, DC: Center for Global Development.

Rakner, L. and N. van de Walle (2009) 'Opposition parties and incumbent presidents: the new dynamics of electoral competition in Africa', in S. I. Lindberg (ed.), *Democratization by Elections: A New Mode of Transition*, Baltimore, MD: Johns Hopkins University Press, pp. 202–25.

Rocha Menocal, A. (2011) 'Analysing the relationship between democracy and development: defining basic concepts and assessing key linkages', in Commonwealth Secretariat (ed.), *Commonwealth Good Governance 2011/12*, London: Nexus Strategic Partnerships, pp. 17–27.

Rocha Menocal, A. and B. Sharma (2008) *Joint Evaluation of Citizens' Voice and Accountability: Synthesis Report*, London: DfID.

Rodrik, D. (2007a) 'Getting institutions right', in D. Rodrik (ed.), *One Economics, Many Recipes: Globalization, Institutions, and Economic Growth*, Princeton, NJ: Princeton University Press, pp. 184–92.

— (2007b) 'Institutions for high-quality growth', in D. Rodrik (ed.), *One Economics, Many Recipes: Globalization, Institutions, and Economic Growth*, Princeton, NJ: Princeton University Press, pp. 153–83.

— (2008) 'Second-best institutions', *American Economic Review*, 98(2): 100–104.

Roll, M. (2011) 'Can "pockets of effectiveness" trigger public sector transformation in Africa?', Paper presented at the 4th European Conference on African Studies, Uppsala, 15–18 June.

Rondinelli, D. A. (1983) *Development Projects as Policy Experiments: An Adaptive Approach to Development Administration*, London: Methuen.

Rothstein, B. (2011) *The Quality of Government: Corruption, Social Trust, and Inequality in International Perspective*, Chicago, IL: Chicago University Press.

Sabiti, B. and A. K. Ssebunya (2012) '"What works for the poor": local governance systems and the delivery of maternal health, water and sanitation in two rural districts of Uganda', Background Paper 16, London: Africa Power and Politics Programme/ Development Research and Training.

Saito, F. (ed.) (2008) *Foundations for Local Governance: Decentralization in Comparative Perspective*, Heidelberg: Physica-Verlag.

Sandbrook, R. (1985) *The Politics of Africa's Economic Stagnation*, Cambridge: Cambridge University Press.

Sandler, T. (1992) *Collective Action: Theory and Applications*, New York: Harvester-Wheatsheaf.

Shivakumar, S. (2005) *The Constitution of Development: Crafting Capabilities for Self-Governance*, New York: Palgrave Macmillan.

Smoke, P. (2003) 'Decentralisation in Africa: goals, dimensions, myths and challenges', *Public Administration and Development*, 23: 7–16.

Soreide, T., A. Tostensen and I. A. Skage (2012) *Hunting for Per Diem: The Uses and Abuses of Travel Compensation in Three Developing Countries*, Oslo: Norad Evaluation Department.

Ssebunya, A. K. (2010) 'Public goods delivery in Uganda: Exploring local governance forms and leadership that work for the poor', Paper presented at the APPP Local Governance Research Stream Workshop, Paris.

Swidler, A. (1986) 'Culture in action: symbols and strategies', *American Sociological Review*, 51: 273–86.

Swidler, A. and S. Cotts Watkins (2009) '"Teach a man to fish": the sustainability doctrine and its social consequences', *World Development*, 37(7): 1182–96.

Therkildsen, O. (1988) *Watering White Elephants? Lessons from Donor Funded Planning and Implementation of Water Supplies in Tanzania*, Uppsala: Scandinavian Institute of African Studies.

— (2000) 'Public sector reform in a poor, aid-dependent country, Tanzania', *Public Administration and Development*, 20: 61–71.

— (2012) 'Policy making and implementation in agriculture: Tanzania's push for irrigated rice', DIIS/EPP Working Paper 2011:26, Copenhagen: Danish Institute for International Studies.

Therkildsen, O. and F. Bourgouin (2012) 'Continuity and change in Tanzania's ruling coalition: legacies, crises and weak productive capacity', DIIS/EPP Working Paper 2012:06, Copenhagen: Danish Institute for International Studies.

Titeca, K. and T. de Herdt (2011) 'Real governance beyond the "failed state": negotiating education in the Democratic Republic of the Congo', *African Affairs*, 110(439): 213–31.

Treisman, D. (2007) *The Architecture of Government: Rethinking Political Decentralization*, Cambridge: Cambridge University Press.

UBOS and ICF International (2012) *Uganda Demographic and Health Survey 2011*, Kampala: Uganda Bureau of Statistics and ICF International.

Uganda, Republic of (2010) *Millennium Development Goals Report for Uganda 2010: Special Theme – Accelerating Progress towards Improving Maternal Health*, Kampala: Ministry of Finance, Planning and Economic Development.

UN ESCAP (n.d.) 'What is good governance?', United Nations Economic and Social Commission for Asia and the Pacific, www.unescap.org/pdd/prs/ProjectActivities/Ongoing/gg/governance.asp, accessed 28 December 2012.

UNFPA (2012) 'Sub-Saharan Africa's maternal death rate down 41 per cent', UN Fund for Population Activities, africa.unfpa.org/public/cache/offonce/news/pid/10767, accessed 22 December 2012.

UN-Habitat (2011) *Malawi: Blantyre Urban Profile*, Nairobi: United Nations Human Settlements Programme.

Unsworth, S. (2009) 'What's politics got to do with it? Why donors find it so hard to come to terms with politics, and why this matters', *Journal of International Development*, 21(6): 883–94.

Uvin, P. (1998) *Aiding Violence: The Development Enterprise in Rwanda*, West Hartford, CT: Kumarian Press.

Vajja, A. and H. White (2008) 'Can the World Bank build social capital? The experience of social funds in Malawi and Zambia', *Journal of Development Studies*, 44(8): 1145–68.

van de Walle, N. (2001) *African Economies and the Politics of Permanent Crisis, 1979–1999*, Cambridge: Cambridge University Press.

— (2007) 'Meet the new boss, same as the old boss? Evolution of political clientelism in Africa', in H. Kitschelt and S. I. Wilkinson (eds), *Patrons, Clients, and Policies: Patterns of Democratic Accountability and Politi-*

cal Competition, Cambridge: Cambridge University Press, pp. 50–67.

van Donge, J. K., D. Henley and P. Lewis (2012) 'Tracking development in Southeast Asia and sub-Saharan Africa: the primacy of policy', Development Policy Review, 30(S1): s5–s24.

Vandemoortele, J. (2009) 'The MDG conundrum: meeting the targets without missing the point', Development Policy Review, 27(4): 355–71.

Vangeenderhuysen, C., J.-P. Banos and T. Mahaman (1995) 'Mortalité maternale évitable en milieu urbain à Niamey (Niger)', Cahiers Santé, 5(49–54).

Villalón, L. A. and M. Bodian (2012) 'Religion, demande sociale, et réformes éducatives au Senegal', Research Report 05, London: Africa Power and Politics Programme.

Villalón, L. and M. Tidjani-Alou (2012) Religion and Education in Africa: Harnessing Religious Values to Developmental Ends, Policy Brief 07, London: Africa Power and Politics Programme.

Villalón, L. A., A. Idrissa and M. Bodian (2012) 'Religion, demande sociale, et réformes éducatives au Niger', Research Report 06, London: Africa Power and Politics Programme.

Vlasblom, D. (2013) The Richer Harvest: The 'Tracking Development' Study 2006–2011, Leiden: African Studies Centre.

Weber, M. (1978 [1922]) Economy and Society, vol. 2, Berkeley: University of California Press.

Wheeler, C. and A. Leftwich (2012) Coalitions in the Politics of Development: Findings, Insights and Guidance from the DLP Coalitions Workshop. Sydney, 15–16 Feb 2012, Canberra: Developmental Leadership Program.

Whitfield, L. (2011a) 'Growth without economic transformation: economic impacts of Ghana's political settlement', DIIS Working Paper 2011:28, Copenhagen: Danish Institute for International Studies.

— (2011b) 'Competitive clientelism, easy financing and weak capitalists: the contemporary political settlement in Ghana', DIIS/EPP Working Paper 2011:27, Copenhagen: Danish Institute for International Studies.

Whitfield, L. and O. Therkildsen (2011) 'What drives states to support the development of productive sectors? Strategies ruling elites pursue for political survival and their policy implications', DIIS Working Paper 2011:15, Copenhagen: Danish Institute for International Studies.

WHO (2004) 'Reducing maternal and newborn mortality in Africa', African Health Monitor, 5(1): 5–7.

— (2007) WHO Recommended Interventions for Improving Maternal and Newborn Health, Geneva: World Health Organization.

— (n.d.) 'Maternal Mortality Ratio (per 100,000 live births)', World Health Organization, www.who.int/health info/statistics/indmaternalmortality/ en/index.html, accessed 28 December 2012.

WHO, UNICEF, UNFPA and World Bank (2012) Trends in Maternal Mortality 1990 to 2010: WHO, UNICEF, UNFPA and the World Bank Estimates, New York: World Health Organization.

Workman, A. (2011a) 'The politics of public goods provision in post-conflict Makeni, Sierra Leone', Working Paper 15, London: Africa Power and Politics Programme.

— (2011b) 'Makeni City Council and the politics of co-production in post-conflict Sierra Leone', IDS Bulletin, 42(2): 53–63.

World Bank (1997) World Development Report 1997: The State in a Changing World, Washington, DC: Oxford University Press/World Bank.

— (2003) *World Development Report 2004: Making Services Work for Poor People*, Washington, DC: Oxford University Press/World Bank.
— (2012) 'The Global Partnership for Social Accountability: a new mechanism to support civil society organizations', web.worldbank.org/WBSITE/EXTERNAL/NEWS/0,,content MDK:23175490~pag PK:34370~piPK:34424~theSitePK:4607,00. html, accessed 16 August 2012.

INDEX

abortion, 42

absenteeism of staff in healthcare, 57, 62

accountability, 1, 8, 9, 13–14, 19, 85, 99, 104, 120, 133; in Rwanda, 65; 'long route' of, 25; social, 26–9, 30, 69, 126, 132

adaptive approaches, 129

Africa Power and Politics Programme (APPP), 2, 6, 11, 12, 16, 19, 20, 36, 38, 39, 40, 57, 66, 70, 74, 77, 82, 85, 86, 89, 95, 97, 99, 100, 107, 110, 113, 138; fieldwork, 31, 45, 46, 90, 116; Local Governance and Leadership team, 2, 50, 58, 73; working papers, 131

aid: potential harm done by, 120; realism about, 137; suspicions about, 123

Alternative Dispute Resolution (ADR), 110–11

ambulances, 59–60; provision of, 118 (in Niger, 52–3, 78; in Rwanda, 54); stretcher-ambulances, 54

antenatal care, 42, 48, 50, 51

anti-corruption action, 1, 15, 16, 70, 127

associational models, aid-driven, 115–16

Bamako Initiative, 79

Banda, Joyce, 34

Bangalore, citizens' score-cards experiment, 26

Belgian Technical Cooperation (BTC), 119, 121

'best fit' approach, 10–11, 96, 124

'best practice', 10–11, 124

bio-medical field, improvements in, 122

Blantyre (Malawi), city administration in, 75–6

Blantyre Water Board (BWB), 91

blockages and bottlenecks: in maternal healthcare, 41, 42–3, 47, 58, 59, 62, 66, 78; in public goods provision, 2, 6–7, 19, 74, 80, 95, 97, 128

burial societies, 103

bwalo justice, 107–10, 117, 131

Caesarean section, 46, 47; free of charge, 60; shortage of kits for, 56

capacity, development of, 136

Catholic church, 112

chiefs, 34, 35, 78, 94, 104, 105, 106, 107, 108; advisers of (*nduna*), 109; defined jurisdictions of, 110; ill-defined powers of, 75–6; use of enforcers, 107 *see also* town chiefs

China, economic rise of, 3

cholera, 77

churches: provision of alternative healthcare, 46; provision of education, 112

Citizenship DRC, *Blurring the Boundaries*, 27

civil society, building of, 115, 123, 134

client power, 24–6, 30, 132

clientelism, 25, 33, 82–3, 86, 88, 94, 134; competitive, 94–5

co-production of public goods, 74

coffee, marketing of, 39

coherence of policy *see* policy coherence

collective action, 15, 16, 18, 103, 104; elite barriers to, 96; in relation to elections, 89–90; problems of, 41, 73, 88, 97, 101, 107, 114–15, 120, 125 (in Malawi, 102–10); realism in, 130–2; requires skills and experience, 102

Commission on Human Rights and Administrative Justice (CHRAJ) (Ghana), 111, 132

Common Development Fund (CDF) (Rwanda), 61

commons: destruction of, 18; tragedy of, 17, 104

Community Health Workers (CHW)

(Rwanda), 49, 57–8, 64; incentivisa-
tion of, 64–5
complaints about antisocial behaviour,
103
complex change, facilitation of, 135–9
confused mandates, problem of, 74
Congo, Democratic Republic of (DRC),
37, 40, 96
context, importance of, 98–9
convening and brokering, 133, 139
corruption, 9, 32, 33, 82, 84–5, 100, 122
see also anti-corruption action
cost recovery, in maternal healthcare, 43
costs of healthcare, 42
courts of law, 107–10; customary,
111; traditional, 108; use of local
languages in, 108
Crisis States Centre, London School of
Economics, 87
cultural commonalities, 100
curfews, 106, 107
Cyanika health centre, Rwanda, 57

decentralisation, 79, 85, 91, 123; critique
of, 22–3; democratic, 22–4, 30, 126,
132; in healthcare provision, 61, 69
demand, rediscovering of, 24–6
demand-side approaches to governance
reform, 12–13, 73, 104, 105, 126, 127,
139
democracy, 1, 13, 32, 88, 96, 130;
African, 73 (nature of, 19; as help or
hindrance, 84–90; weak source for
performance, 84); and collective
action, 89–90; contextualisation
of, 86–9; deepening of, 134;
effectiveness of, 87; local, 85;
participatory, 91; requires
economic development, 86, 123;
requires institutions, 123; safe
for development, 133–5 *see also*
decentralisation, democratic
Democratic Progressive Party (DPP)
(Malawi), 91, 92
Demographic and Health Surveys (DHS),
43–4
Department for International
Development (DfID) (UK), 124, 135

development: business of, 1, 3; focus on
obtaining aid, 136; in Africa, status of,
3–4; rents deriving from, 114
Development Research and Training
(DRT), 39–40
Developmental Leadership Programme,
20
devolution of resources and decisions,
22
disease, 6; diarrhoeal, 77; reduction of, 5
DNV organisation, 113
doctors, salaries of, 64
donor funding, 114, 120; influence of,
136 (on East African pastoralists,
116; perverse, 101, 138); undermines
collective action, 132
donor policy agendas, 101, 115–16;
influence on public sector reform, 80

education: in healthcare, 45, 48–51;
public, design of, 111–12
elections, 1, 32, 33, 35, 87, 92, 123; careless
promotion of, 87; effectiveness of,
89; in Malawi, postponement of, 85;
multi-party, 86, 90–5
elite incentives, as 'black box', 19
elite politics, and development, 126
Elites, Production and Poverty project,
20
empowerment of citizens, 13, 14, 24–6,
30, 104, 125, 126
enforcement of healthcare provision, in
Rwanda, 50
enterprise environment, 2
ethnicity, importance of, 100
extra pennies initiative (Niger), 52–3, 66,
118–19, 120, 129, 133; banned, 52

family planning services, access to, 42
food security, ring-fencing of, 135
fragmentation, 97; of municipal
authority, 75; of political elites, 86,
96; social, 101, 102–4
free-rider problem, 17, 69, 88, 104–5;
control of, 18
Future State Centre, 27

game theory, 100

Ghana, 40, 95–6, 101; associational tax in, 82; local justice in, 100, 110–11, 132

girls, education of, 112

governance: for development, 122–5; 'good', 1, 4, 9–30, 58, 86, 96, 115, 123–4, 136, 139 (definition of, 9); 'that works', 9–30

Green, Duncan, 133, 139

growth, jobless, 3

Habyarimana, Juvenal, 37, 38, 67

healthcare, primary, free, 78–9 see also maternal healthcare

Health Centre Committee (Ndirande, Malawi), 55–6

health centres, location of, 61

health insurance, 49, 51, 53–4, 119 see also mutuelle de santé

health services, modern, use of, 42, 45–51

Health Surveillance Assistants (HSAs) (Malawi), 76

'hedge-clipping' of hard-working individuals, 83–4

heterogeneity, 97

HIV/AIDS, 48; in Uganda, 40; self-help in Malawi, 116; testing for, 50

homogeneity, social, 131

human development, uneven progress in, 4–6

Hutu people, 37

hybrid institutions, construction of, 69

hybridity, practical, 99–101, 120, 129; in West Africa, 110–12

illiteracy, 85, 102

imihigo performance contracts, 65

incentives, perverse, problem of, 74, 97

incumbents, power of, 90

information-sharing, deficient, 97, 125

infrastructure investments, ring-fencing of, 135

'Inkatha' vigilantes, 106

innumeracy, 102, 103

Institute of Development Studies, 20

institutional incoherence, 95

institutional monocropping, 10

institutionalisation, from bottom up, 119, 133

institutions: as resources for reform, 99; built from scratch, 101

islands of effectiveness see pockets of effectiveness

Issoufou, Mahamadou, 36

justice, local, in Ghana, 100, 110–11, 132 see also bwalo justice

Kagame, Paul, 37, 70

Kamuzu Banda, Hastings, 33, 78, 83–4, 90, 108; legacies of, 94–5

Kayibanda, Grégoire, 37

Kelsall, Tim, 31, 32, 99, 100, 112, 128

Kenya, 40

Khan, M., 126

Laboratoire d'Études et de Recherche sur les Dynamiques Sociales et le Développement Local (LASDEL) (Niger), 36, 83

life expectancy, 33, 35, 36, 39

limited access order (LAO), 32

local problem-solving, 97–121; barriers to, 101–2; in maternal healthcare, 66–8; in Niger, 113–16; realising potential of, 132–3

local reforms, enabling of, 116–20

magic, 47; belief in, 46

'magic bullets', 126; problem of, 21–9

Malawi, 33–4, 73–4, 83–4, 101, 129, 131; AIDS self-help in, 116; collective action challenges in, 102–10; maternal health provision in, 45–6 (quality of, 55–6); private healthcare in, 53; problem-solving in, 117

Malawi Congress Party (MCP), 91, 92, 94

Mali, 40; education in, 112

marabouts, use of, 47

markets, management of, 2, 73, 113; in Ndirande (Malawi), 90–3, 131

maternal healthcare: comparative delivery of, 41–72; coordination of, 74; quality of, 54–8

maternal mortality, 41–2; causes of, 42–3; uncertainty of data regarding, 43; viewed as fate, 46–7
medicine, traditional, 46
merit goods, 6; definition of, 7
middle class, small size of, 1
Millennium Development Goals (MDGs), 4–5, 41
mistrust in communities, 102–4
monetary policy, ring-fencing of, 135
monitoring of public services, 18, 126
motherhood, safe, as Millennium Development Goal, 41 *see also* maternal healthcare
Muluzi, Bakili, 33–4, 83, 92
Museveni, Yoweri, 39
Mutharika, Bingu wa, 34, 46, 83, 91, 92
Mutharika, Peter, 34
mutuelle de santé, 49, 51, 53–4, 65

Nasolo river (Malawi), management of, 76–8, 104–6, 131
National Resistance Movement (NRM), 39
Ndirande (Blantyre, Malawi), 34, 55, 75–8, 102–10, 117, 131; fire in market, 92; market management in, 92–3
Neighbourhood Watch groups, 106–7, 117; training of guards, 107
neopatrimonialism, 32, 70, 82, 84, 88, 123
Niger, 35–6, 73, 83, 101, 129; ambulance provision in, 52–3; education in, 112; local problem-solving in, 113–16; local reforms in, 118; maternal mortality in, 46–7; policy coherence in, 59–61; quality of maternal healthcare in, 56; unresolved policy conflicts in, 78–9
non-excludability, 17
non-governmental organisations (NGOs), 69, 115, 116, 133, 134
North, D. C., 126, 128
nurses: allowance scams, 55; complaints about, 46, 47, 55; 'untouchable', 62
Nyamagabe (Rwanda), 38, 51, 57, 64

Operation Turquoise, 38
Ostrom, E., 97, 98, 101, 114

'our turn to eat' syndrome, 134
overlapping jurisdictions, problem of, 74, 75

Pakistan, collective action in, 114
participation, 13, 31; as watchword, 21
patrimonialism, developmental, 70 *see also* neopatrimonialism
per diems, hunt for, 114
performance disciplines, in maternal healthcare, 62–6
pockets of effectiveness, 81, 82
policing, 107, 131; outsourcing of, 82
policy coherence, 127, 128; in maternal healthcare, 59–61; politics of, 73–96 (examined, 74–80)
politics, as source of livelihood, 130
populist policy initiatives, pursuit of, 80
poverty: reduction of, 3, 4, 9, 137; solutions for, 122; time-consuming nature of, 102
Prevention of Mother to Child Transmission programme, 48, 50
principal-agent approach, 3, 8, 11–14, 19, 58, 84, 101, 125, 126, 133, 135, 139; definition of, 11; shedding of, 14–19
private healthcare, 52, 63; controls on, 64
privatisation of public service provision, 21, 74, 81, 82
programmes, require measurable results, 136–7
provider indiscipline, politics of, 73–96 (examined, 80–4)
public expenditure tracking surveys (PETS), 18
public goods: as privilege, not as right, 85; become club goods, 94; concept of, 6; definition of, 7, 17; provision of, 4–6 (causes of problems in, 79–80); understood in broad sense, 6 *see also* blockages and bottlenecks, in public goods provision
public order, provision of, 73, 106–7
publishing of budget information, 26
punishable offences in maternal healthcare, 50–1

Quality of Government Institute, University of Gothenburg, 15–16, 127
quality of healthcare, shortcomings in, 42–3

resources, shortage of, 80
ring-fencing of public goods provision, 135
Rothstein, Bo, 15
Rwanda, 36–8, 82, 129; emergency healthcare in, 53–4; healthcare education in, 48–51; impact of aid on, 116; maternal healthcare in, 41–72 (efficiency in, 57–8; progress in, 68–71); monitoring of development assistance in, 61; policy coherence in, 59–61; political settlement in, 70; power-sharing in, 134–5; rigour in implementation of policies in, 63; strength of national vision in, 71
Rwandan Patriotic Front (RPF), 37

sanitation, public provision of, 2, 73, 76, 102, 113, 116
de Sardan, Olivier, 21, 100, 113–14, 115–16, 132
savings clubs, 103, 109
score-cards for community monitoring, 125
second-best options, 10
security, public, provision of, 73, 106–7
self-help, 99, 101, 103, 116
Senegal, 40; education in, 112
Shivakumar, S., 99, 101
Sierra Leone, 40
silo working, 14
smallholder agriculture, 122
squatter settlements, 78, 106
staffing, shortages of, 56–7, 62, 78; in Niger, 62
state, withdrawal from public service provision, 79, 82
structural adjustment, 35, 39
supply-side approaches to governance reform, 12–13, 69
Swidler, A., 100

'tall-poppy syndrome', 83

Tandja, Mamadou, 35, 59, 60, 78
Tanzania, 40, 96, 101, 107
taxation, 75, 78; outsourcing of, 82
templates, failure of, 120
timeliness of emergency treatment, 42, 51
town chiefs, 117
trade unions, 82
traditional birth attendants (TBAs), 48; banning of, 45, 48, 51; preference for, 46, 53
'translocal' residents, 102, 107
Tuareg revolt in Niger, 35
Tutsi people, 37

ubudehe practices (Rwanda), 67
ubuntu, 105
Uganda, 38–40, 85–6, 96; maternal health provision in, 47–8; private healthcare in, 53; staffing problems in healthcare, 56–7, 62–3
umuganda practices (Rwanda), 67–8
United Democratic Front (UDF) (Malawi), 91, 92
uranium, 35
urbanisation, 33
user charges, 60, 79; exemption from, 43; free services, 63

vertical discipline, 95
Village Health Teams (VHTs) (Uganda), 48
voice, 13, 14, 27, 104
voluntary associations, 115–16
volunteerism, 114
voters, complicit in poor provision, 95

waiting wards for expectant mothers, 54
Wallis, J. J., 126
Washington Consensus, 81
water: depoliticisation of services, 91; pollution of sources of, 77; public provision of, 2, 73, 76
water committees, 113
water kiosks, in Malawi, 90–2, 131
Water Users Associations (WUAs) (Malawi), 91, 102
Weber, Max, 32

Weingast, B. R., 126
witchcraft: accusation of, 109; belief in, 102–3
women, community groups in Kenya, 116
'working with the grain', 99, 110, 130

World Bank, 13, 28, 124, 125, 126, 136; Global Partnership for Social Accountability, 29; Social Funds, 116
World Development Report, *Making Services Work for Poor People*, 23–6

About Zed Books

Zed Books is a critical and dynamic publisher, committed to increasing awareness of important international issues and to promoting diversity, alternative voices and progressive social change. We publish on politics, development, gender, the environment and economics for a global audience of students, academics, activists and general readers. Run as a co-operative, Zed Books aims to operate in an ethical and environmentally sustainable way.

Find out more at:

www.zedbooks.co.uk

For up-to-date news, articles, reviews and events information visit:

http://zed-books.blogspot.com

To subscribe to the monthly Zed Books e-newsletter, send an email headed 'subscribe' to:

marketing@zedbooks.net

We can also be found on **Facebook, ZNet, Twitter** and **Library Thing**.